WITHOUT A FATHER

WITHOUT A FATHER

FROM FEAR TO FAITH

KENNETH JOYNER

NEW DEGREE PRESS

COPYRIGHT © 2019 KENNETH JOYNER

WITHOUT A FATHER

From Fear to Faith

ISBN   978-1-64137-270-1   *Paperback*

978-1-64137-476-7   *Ebook*

This book is dedicated to every person who has grown up
without a father or a strong male presence in their life.

To my life's most precious gift, my daughter
Bria. I am so honored to be your father.

To my queen, Nicole, thank you so much for saving
my life and loving me unconditionally.

Finally, and most importantly to my first love; God.
Thank you for not giving up on me when I was in the
process of becoming who you called me to be. I pray
that in the end, you would be pleased with my life.

CONTENTS

CALLING ALL FATHERS

So I sought for a man among them who would make a wall, and stand in the gap before Me on behalf of the land, that I should not destroy it; but I found no one.

(EZEK 22:30)

Where are our fathers? Where are the strong and courageous men that God and our society are looking for? Gone are the days of traditional families, which were led by strong and courageous men who placed an undying loyalty on family values. Gone are the days when children would meet their fathers at the door after a hard day of work.

These traditional norms have been replaced with the ever-present oxymoron of single mothers and single-family homes. Mothers have been left with the overwhelming task of parenting from a dual role to provide their children with the support, guidance, and training that fathers should provide, while also having to give the unfailing love and nurturing that comes from within. The constant pressure facing mothers and our society of carrying the weight of absent fathers is eroding the core of families and, thus, deteriorating every aspect of our society.

Every day, more than 47 percent of African American children, 23 percent of Hispanic children, 13 percent of Caucasian children, and 7 percent of Asian children go to bed in a single-family home. According to the data derived by Fatherhood.org and the US Census Bureau, 1 in 4 children live without their fathers.

The effects of absent fathers can be felt in every area of our society. Children who grow up with absent fathers are four times more likely to experience poverty, go to prison, and experience behavioral problems. The infant mortality rate more than doubles when fathers are not present. In addition, our daughters are seven times more likely to become pregnant in their teenage years. In short, everything can be traced back to our missing dads.

In an article written in the February 27 issue of U.S. News & World Report, the author concluded that **Dad is Destiny.**

The role of the father can and will determine a child's success and happiness. Before this book could be written, I had to experience the absence of my father, which left me searching in the dark for my own destiny.

My mother, a single mom raising four children by herself, did what most mothers have done for years—the best she could. However, in all her efforts, there was just no way she could teach me how to be a man. In 1988, I was just nineteen years old, the same age my mother was when she had me. One year removed from high school, I faced my first challenge as a male. With no discipline, lost in my arrogance, I began to indulge in a pleasure-seeking lifestyle. One day, the young lady I was dating said the words we both knew were possible but didn't want to hear — "I'm pregnant." When you're not really a man, those words often frighten you and make you feel inadequate.

I was so afraid and unprepared to be a father that I allowed that fear to lead us to have an abortion. I will have to live with this decision for the rest of my life, and it is one of my greatest failures as a man. Abortion. The word itself leaves an empty hole in my soul. I believe every man is called to be the foundation on which his family is built, unfortunately, on this day, I didn't answer the call. Even to this day, it makes me bow my head in shame and regret. When you're young, you never think you'll get another chance to fix the mistakes you made. It's only when you get older that you truly appreciate second chances.

When my wife told me in 1995 that we were pregnant, I was overjoyed. I felt God was giving me a second chance to right the wrong I had done. In my heart, I thought God would give me a son so I could be a better father to him than my father had been to me. However, as my great-grandmother always said, "God may not give us what we want, but he always gives us what we need." I got what I needed—a beautiful, healthy daughter. God had fulfilled the first part of my purpose in life; he designed me to be a father. From that moment on, I've been on a continuous journey to right the wrong I committed. This has led me to champion a cause greater than myself.

BUILDING STRONG MEN

Can men save the world? I believe they can. To some, it may seem like an impossible task. However, with patience, consistency, and faith, I believe we can change the tide and move in a new direction that will change this world for the better.

Patience. Even the word itself can be scary for some. It means we must resist the desire to give up on men who have experienced pain, disappointment, and failure in being a man and a father. We must give them time to apply the principles of truth that will lead them to become the best version of themselves. The world is plagued with men who lack character, integrity, discipline, and a moral fiber, who will stand in the face of injustice. Weak men continue to lead in ways, which are both ineffective and unproductive for our current and future society.

Frederick Douglass said, "It's easier to build strong children than to repair broken men." What he's saying is that once a man is set in his pattern of governing and operating his life, it is nearly impossible for him to change and transform himself beyond his innate habits and thinking.

Typically, fatherhood is seen from a biological perspective, but fatherhood is about equipping our children with the principles and skills needed to become productive adults. Young people are suffering every day because they do not have the skills needed to navigate successfully in an extremely unsympathetic world. The overall push is to return to the nuclear family structure, and, in theory, all our problems would be solved. However, that won't make a difference in the lives of young people who are currently living apart or disconnected from their fathers.

As a child, I was broken. I couldn't understand why I had to endure so much pain, both physically and mentally. Not having my father in my life left an indelible mark on my soul. His absence both angered me and left me confused about who

I was and why I had to live under the constant cover of suffering. I've learned from my 50 years on this planet that our young people need practical skills that will ultimately help them change their behavior and lead them in the direction of their purpose and destiny. Building strong men can only be done when we are intentional about developing, guiding, and training them from an early age to reach for the greatness that lies within every man.

ALL THINGS WORK TOGETHER

In my early years and well into my thirties, I kept asking myself, "What is the point of it all?" Why did I have to endure so much pain, trauma, adversity, and disappointment? When I became a teacher, I knew it was my chance to give back and make a difference in the lives of young people every day. I knew it would be a difficult challenge, but one I was eager to take on.

After my first week of school in my first year of teaching, it all made sense to me. There I was teaching kids who were experiencing some of the same things I had lived through. It gave me an insight, which revealed the true motives of many of their behaviors. It was not that they disrespected me, but it was a loud cry for help because of what many of them were coping with even before they came to school. I had been given a gift through the training of trauma and real-life experiences, which would allow me to become increasingly effective in reaching even the most difficult children. In 2016, I was given a chance to put all I had been through into practice when I helped develop a non-profit called, ironically, Boys With a Purpose. Although I don't have a son, I have been a father figure for hundreds of young men.

The effects of fatherlessness can be seen in homes, schools, hospitals, and prisons. It is completely impossible to describe the magnitude of the role of the father and his impact on society. Vilifying or condemning absent fathers won't change the current state of society. Many men have fallen from grace because they lack the principles or the keys to unlock their true purpose in life. The solution doesn't lie solely in reconnecting biological fathers with their children (although that would be ideal), but it hinges on training young people to effectively navigate successfully in this world.

Imagine a world of men who had integrity, discipline, values, and self-worth and who kept their word and honored all women—men who were able to lead with the power and authority given to them by God. Imagine these men as effective leaders in their homes, schools, churches, and communities. What if we could train up a generation of men who embody what God intended for them to be? How would that change the world?

Everyone is talking about the crisis of absent fathers, but no one has written a solution. By taking the most tragic and challenging moments of my life and learning from them, I was able to survive a devastating home life filled with domestic violence, drug-infested neighborhoods, and a slew of life-changing tragedies. These experiences have been crafted into this book to give you the real-life principles that can be applied in anyone's life and will train our youth and guide them from boys to men.

Principles function like formulas that, when applied correctly, always lead to success. Principles don't discriminate. They transcend race, ethnicity, and socioeconomic status. Principles override all factors and level the playing field for everyone.

THE CALL

The role of a father is constantly being redefined, and mediocrity has become the standard of success for many. There is a *call for men and fathers* who will dare to resist punching the absentee ballot of fatherhood and cast a living sacrificial vote to become the great men and fathers they were designed to be. God is looking for men who will build a protective hedge around their families and stand in the gap against all depravity for their children. Without strong men and fathers in place, we leave the doors of frustration, immorality, confusion, and darkness open, allowing them to destroy the future for our children.

I believe we've lost the human connection with our children and left them with no foundation for the future. If more men don't serve as role models and be present for their children, the next three generations will be lost. Men, the time is now to stand and lead!

This book speaks directly to men, fathers, boys, girls, and single mothers. My goal is to give each of these groups practical tools and principles that will help unlock the full potential that lives within us all. I also want to give a solid foundation to every young man who has ever felt alone or burdened by the absence of his father. If we can empower all men to properly train, teach, and live out these principles for our youth, we can create a better future for us all.

For every young man or woman who has grown up without a father, or any parent raising a child who doesn't have a relationship with his/her father, this book will give you practical principles that can be applied by anyone to achieve more success in life. Teachers, counselors, parents, grandparents, and those struggling with their own fatherless childhoods will be able to see how adversity can and will eventually lead to success. It will give you insight into how all pain, trials, and problems can be traced back to fundamental principles that ultimately hold the key to success. The call is for every man to stand and help equip our youth with a complete understanding of who they are and what they can become. This will give them the power to resist the temptation to throw their lives away.

PART I

IN THE BEGINNING

CHAPTER 1

JUST LIKE YOUR FATHER

———

Often, I go back as far as I can to try to remember where it all began. It always brings me back to the same moment, which plays repeatedly in my mind every day. Through the paper walls of our two-bedroom apartment, there is yelling and screaming coming from the bedroom. Things are being thrown around, and I can hear the screams of desperation from my mom, each louder than the next. I plant my ear against the door, wishing there was something I could do to save her. I begin to use what my great-grandmother called "liquid prayers" — tears only God can hear. From my soul, I cry out and ask him to save her, but it never happens.

The door flings open and I fall through, only to see my stepfather standing over me. Behind the overturned furniture, the lamp casts a silhouette on my mom. I can see her crying;

even more, I can feel the pain cascading down her face with every tear. Then, with an anger I had often seen before, my stepfather grabs me and slams me against the wall. With my feet dangling in the air and his forearm pressed against my chest, he looks at me with an unstoppable rage and says, "*You just like your father*; you ain't never going to be nothing!"

As I scream for my dad, those cries go unanswered. In an instant, I feel the air leaving my body and, for a moment, I'm gone. Then suddenly, I'm pulled back by the screams of my mom, and he turns his anger from me to her. What he said left a stain on my brain, and I would spend the next thirty years of my life trying to kill that voice in my head that told me I could never be anything. We would experience even greater pain, and before it was over, I would see my mom beaten to within an inch of her life. This was our life, and this is my story.

358

"The future has a way of arriving unannounced"

– GEORGE F. WILL

When I was young, one of my deepest fears was being alone. Being alone left me to my memories and all the mental and physical abuse my mom and I had endured. It made me think back to the abusive times in my life when I did not believe we would ever survive.

I was born on February 12, 1969, and my father wasn't there. His best friend, Kenny Pawham, took my mother to the hospital and, because of that, my mother named me after him. A few days later, my father arrived at the hospital to see me. Unfortunately, I have no memories of those times.

Being broken would be the theme in my life for quite some time. One day, unexpected and unannounced to me on February 5, 1970, my future met my present and my father was shipped off to fight in the Vietnam War. In an instant, after just 358 days of being in this world, half of who I was had gone. I didn't know then that it wasn't his choice, but his absence would have a profound effect on the *man* I would become.

I was raised, in my opinion by some of the most dynamic women in the world. Born to the oldest of seven girls, I was the first male child the family had ever seen. This distinction brought me great praise and notoriety. In other words, I was spoiled rotten. My grandfather was extremely excited about my arrival because, for some time, he was the only male surrounded by eight women, which included my grandmother.

His presence still lives with me today. He was a man's man; you could count on him and his word truly meant something.

He was never confused about who he was or his role as a man in our family. Naturally, I looked to him to define myself as a man. I observed and admired just how he carried himself both in good times and in bad. I trusted his opinion and respected his judgment. In short, I believed in him as a true role model, and he became my father at that time.

My early years were spent living between two places, my great grandmother's house on F. St. N.E. and my grandfather's house in River Terrace. How my grandparents made it in a two-bedroom, one-bathroom home with eight women and just my grandfather was simply amazing. As kids, my friends and I would go out to the parkway and watch the cars go by, and sometimes we threw rocks at them. You could see what used to be RFK Stadium from the back windows of the house.

One day, my grandfather rushed into the house with excitement to announce that we were going to a game. I couldn't believe it. I was so happy! When we arrived, I got my first taste of cotton candy. You can't imagine what that was like. It was here that I would be allowed to make one of my first choices in life without fear. The vendor walked up to us with a tray of small flags, one with the Redskins logo and one with the Dallas logo—guess which one I chose. I'll let you know later. My only regret is that I never took the time to take him to a game when I got older.

"You're special, and you're going to do something with your life"

These are the words, my family, especially my grandfather and my aunts, echoed to me daily. They never let me forget how special I was. That seed, planted deep within my psyche, helped push me to strive to be the best at whatever I did. It also gave me a weapon to fight against what had previously been programmed in my psyche. My great-grandmother was the rock of our family. It seemed to me that with everything going on in the world, she had the one true connection to God that no one else could understand. How she carried herself under the anointing of God made him real to me.

In addition to having a spiritual foundation like none other, she also had a human side. Nothing was more important than family. She believed in the strength and integrity of what family stood for. This drove her to do everything she could to keep it intact.

I went to live with her when I was five, and it seemed my life was getting better. These were the happiest times of my life. She made sure I started school on time and that I understood that no matter what, education would be my way out of a life of abuse and poverty. I know this is where I got my first introduction to God. We had to get up early every Sunday to load up the car with pots and pans to head to Springfield Baptist

Church, where my grandmother would cook breakfast to feed the whole church. This is where I learned to serve others. During the summers, I was moved back and forth from my great-grandmother's house to my grandfather's home, but I still had moments with my mom. Even though I hated my stepfather, I loved being with my mom. We would always have a special bond that could never be broken.

I have structured this book around twenty core principles of being a father figure, which isn't necessarily about being the biological father (although it can be), but it's about playing the role of a father figure. These principles will be called W.O.W for Words of Wisdom.

W.O.W. #1 KNOW WHO YOU ARE

God spoke: "Let us make human beings in our image, make them reflecting our nature So they can be responsible for the fish in the sea, the birds in the air, the cattle, And, yes, Earth itself, and every animal that moves on the face of Earth." God created human beings; he created them godlike, Reflecting God's nature. He created them male and female.

(GEN 1:26-27)

I didn't learn this until late in life. I thought I was a failure. I thought I wasn't good enough. I believed something was wrong with me and that every bad situation was somehow my fault. After I felt abandoned, rejected, and orphaned, I learned that you and I are made in the image of God.

We have the same characteristics as our Father in heaven. I know now that voice in my head echoing my stepfather's words, "You just like your father," wasn't a death sentence—it was an affirmation of the truth laid out in my destiny. When people use your biological father to refer to the negative aspects of your character, God wants to remind you that he made you first in his image. That means you are perfect just the way you are. You matter and you are more than enough.

Some things will be out of your control. However, even if your biological father isn't in your life, your spiritual father will never leave you or forget the things that are important to you. No matter what, trust God and walk in his ways. He will have the final say in what happens in your life. **Don't waste time. Read God's Word and find out who you really are and where he wants to take you. Say this daily—I matter, and I am more than enough!**

- **You are valuable** – *Genesis 2:7: "I am the creator and you are my creation. I breathed into your nostrils the breath of life."* God will always take care of what he created. We are his greatest creation and he wants nothing more than for us to be successful in what he created us for.

- **You have God's Spirit** – *Luke 8:21: You not only have a new father but also a new family of brothers and sisters.* Surround yourself with those who have the same spirit that leads to God. Your spirit is the life force of your body. Just as batteries give life to a flashlight, so does the spirit give life to your body. When you have God's spirit there is nothing you can't do or overcome.

- **You represent God** – *Ephesians 4:1: "Therefore I, a prisoner for serving the Lord, beg you to lead a life worthy of your calling, for you have been called by God."* It's one thing to be called by our friends, parents, or family, but you and I are called by God. We must represent him at all times. The real question is, will you answer the call.

CHAPTER 2

THE BITTER MAN

"Bitterness is like cancer, it eats upon the host. But anger is like fire it burns it all away."

– MAYA ANGELOU

IT'S NOT YOUR FAULT

First, let us kill the lie you might believe about why your father is not involved in your life. That lie tells you that somehow it must be your fault. Self-blame became an emotional abuser that heightened my low self-esteem and made me believe even more that I wasn't good enough. This self-inflicted wound became my weapon of choice whenever I faced difficult situations in my early life. I often felt that something must be wrong with me or that I must have done something to deserve the condition I was in. I was wrong. I hadn't asked to be born. I didn't cause my father not to be in my life. It all came down to choices I had no responsibility for. You have done nothing to cause separation from your father; the responsibility lies on him.

Now, some fathers aren't in their children's lives for various reasons. However, others have chosen not to be present and take responsibility for their actions. Don't blame yourself for things that are out of your control. This does not mean you won't still long for a relationship with your father, but it means the burden to restore it doesn't fall on your shoulders. Do not point the finger of blame at yourself; it's not your fault.

The climate of the '60s was much different in terms of how people related to having children out of wedlock. Nervous and scared out of her mind, my mother reluctantly announced to my grandfather she was pregnant. With my father headed off to fight in the war, there would be no wedding. To avoid the shame and embarrassment of an unwed daughter, my mother was sent to live with my great-grandmother. In 1969, my mother graduated at the age of nineteen from Eastern High School in Washington, DC, one year after having me. As a result of the pressure of having to care for a child by herself and the overwhelming odds that my father would not return, my mother waited just over a year before she married my stepfather on March 21, 1970. Life often moves in cycles.

That same year my brother Bernard was born prematurely, due to the violence of his father. He was named after his father and early on that bothered me. When he was younger he would suffer from seizures and had to medication to reduce them. What was most important was that we were brothers and I never let anyone bother him. Growing up my brother latched on genetically to the work ethic given to him by my mom. He always had a job or two and never let anything stop him from getting what he wanted. Over the years we've had our ups and downs, as all brother do, but I'm proud of the man he has become.

One day when I was about 12, I conjured up the courage to ask my mom why she didn't wait until my father returned? She said, with regret in her eyes, "It was complicated. I wasn't sure if he would ever return or if he even wanted to marry me if he did."

Her decision to move forward began a six-year period of intense pain in our lives. A habitual tug of war would form in my soul between wanting my dad's love and resenting his absence. As every birthday and holiday passed without him, the anger and frustration closed my heart a little more each day. After a while, like most children, I stopped longing and hoping and resolved that he was never coming to see about me. I had decided never to give him or anyone my emotions again.

THE SEED OF VIOLENCE

I never liked my stepfather, and he never liked me. As a result of the hatred he had for me, I suffered years of physical and verbal abuse. His anger often focused on my mom, and when I yelled for him to stop beating her, he often turned his attention to me. I was afraid but would have done anything to take the focus off my mom, which often meant putting myself in harm's way. In those days, there was no such thing as "time out," so I was repeatedly beaten.

One night, the explosion of violence reached a boiling point, which convinced my mom to leave him for good. While watching TV with my back toward him, my stepfather approached me in a rage and punched me several times in my head. I was knocked unconscious and rushed to the hospital. Reluctantly, my mom called my grandfather and great-grandmother, and when they arrived, my great-grandmother was heartbroken. When I was five, I went to live with her.

The seed of violence was planted early in my life. Growing up in and around so much violence in the home, you never really know how your heart, mind, and spirit will be affected. When the seeds of violence are planted, they have the potential to produce a devastating form of brutality that can break the soul of its victim. The hate I felt when I saw my mom broken at the hands of my stepfather planted a different kind of seed in my spirit. It made me never want to see any women suffer the emotional and physical abuse I witnessed, but it left me with a burning fire of anger that had the potential to turn me into the very person I didn't want to become.

I think domestic violence should be an oxymoron, just like a "single mother." According to the World Health Organization, domestic violence has increased steadily every year. Today, one in three women will experience domestic violence in their lifetime. In addition, women who are young and have low levels of education are more likely to experience domestic violence. Every nine seconds in the US, a woman is beaten and/or assaulted. I dare to say things are not getting better, but worse. Every year, more than three million children witness domestic violence in their homes. They say boys who witness domestic violence are more likely to commit violence against women in the future. It not only affects mother and child, but it also has damaging repercussions on society. It is the third leading cause for homelessness in the US, but the effects aren't limited to the US—the impact is felt worldwide.

GIFTS FROM PAIN

Fear is birthed in uncertainty, but pure joy often stems from pain. The Bible says a three-strand cord is not easily broken. In September of '74, that three-strand cord was completed when my little sister, Patrice, was born. She was the joy that my mother was hoping for. Her arrival re-energized my mom and added to my responsibility as the oldest child. Together, me, my brother Bernard, and my sister would experience a life no one could imagine. In between taking care of my brother and sister and worrying about my mother, like most children, I often wondered if my father would ever come to see about me. Over time, that longing to be with him and to know his love turned into a slow drip of resentment and bitterness. An absent father will always create a disengaged, fearful byproduct.

W.O.W. #2 LEARN TO FORGIVE

Make every effort to live in peace with everyone and to be holy; without holiness, no one will see the Lord. See to it that no one falls short of the grace of God and that no bitter root grows up to cause trouble and defile many.

(HEB 12:14-15)

All of life's gifts won't come beautifully wrapped and aren't always presented with a smile. Rooted in bitterness is often an unseen gift that will allow you to use the pain and resentment of your situation to produce a tree of forgiveness. Bitterness, at its core, destroys the soul, but forgiveness lights a path of hope for all who dare to embrace it.

It took me a long time to forgive my stepfather for what he did to me and my mom. It took me even longer to forgive my dad for his absence. I'm not saying it will be easy to forgive or that your emotions won't get the best of you at times. I am saying you can't allow your emotions to control all of life's situations. How you feel will change daily, but truth and principles will stand the test of time. It wasn't until later in life that I realized through the enlightenment of God's Word that I had been holding the keys to free myself from my emotional bondage the whole time.

"When you forgive, you heal. When you let go, you grow."

ANONYMOUS

- To have, be, and do all that God plans for your life, you must be whole. You must fill the pits of your heart with his Word and true forgiveness. Letting go of the past hurts and disappointments is the only way to fill the emptiness we feel inside. Unforgiveness is like cancer that grows daily. It eats away at the door of our hearts and kills the one thing we all need to live—**love**.

"The weak can never forgive. Forgiveness is an attribute of the strong"

– MAHATMA GANDHI

- You were born to be free in mind, body, and spirit. Unforgiveness stifles the soul and limits your potential to live a life that can change the world. The more you carry unforgiveness in your heart, the deeper you sink into a life of weakness and mediocrity.

CHAPTER 3

THE BROKEN MAN

Being broken emotionally, physically, and spiritually is not something any of us would sign up for. However, God can use us the most when we're wrapped in our most difficult moments. Even in the midst of trauma, God can produce something that will benefit us in the future.

MOVING ON AND ON

After several years of being battered, my mother finally conjured up the strength to leave my stepfather, and a new journey began for us. You see, while my stepfather wouldn't hurt his own children, he had the capacity to kill me. Finally leaving him freed my spirit and gave me life, but it crippled my brother and sister. To this day, they have no real memory of their father. I never wanted them to hate him as much as

I did, so we never talked about the abuse I witnessed and experienced from him.

A few things really frightened me as a child. I was always afraid one day my mother would prematurely leave me, afraid of my stepfather, and afraid of being alone. I created this tough-guy mentality to hide all the anger I had inside, which prevented fear from overtaking me. However, two words, no matter when I heard them, had the power to break my soul. We learned quickly that on any given day, my mom could come home and say, "We're moving."

By the time we left, I was six, my brother was five, and my sister was one. None of us have pictures with our fathers in our youth. It is as if those days never happened. As a result of the instability in our home, we moved a lot—at least every six months to a year. Initially, it felt like someone had ripped our hearts out and filled them with sadness and disappointment. Eventually, we all became numb and disconnected ourselves emotionally. My brother and I became a professional movers. We would often keep the screws in our bunk beds loose to make it easier to break them down for the next move. Some moves happened in the middle of the night, and some happened just four months into the school year. We could never settle in or get comfortable.

We've lived all over DC and in every part of Prince George's County, Maryland, you can imagine. I'd been to about seven elementary schools, at least four middle schools, and three high schools. During this time, we all suffered under the umbrella of uncertainty and struggled to really trust anyone. Always being the new kid on the block or in the classroom made us feel as though we were on the outside looking in for most of our lives. Now that we are all older, we sometimes play a game to see who can name the most places we've lived. After I went off to college in '89, I lost count.

POVERTY

"Poverty is like being punished for a crime you didn't commit."

– WRITER ELI KHAMAROV

After leaving my stepfather, we faced our second abuser: poverty. As a child, I thought the two richest people in the world were Peter and Paul because every adult I encountered would say they were "robbing Peter to pay Paul."

I learned later it just meant they were broke, in more ways than one. Poverty placed my mom in survival mode. It made every decision for her and drove her to do things she wouldn't normally do.

Just when I thought it couldn't get any worse, we experienced brokenness like never before. One day while attending

William Beanes Elementary, poverty—our second abuser—struck again on the bus ride home. It was a day like any other. The bus was full of loud kids, yelling and hanging out of the windows. The sun was out and I was feeling good, up out of my seat, acting crazy, as all elementary school kids do.

We noticed someone had gotten put out of their apartment, and their stuff was on the side of the road for all to see. Some kids started laughing before the bus stopped, and, ironically, I joined in. Little did I know it was our stuff. As the bus came to a stop, I noticed my mother on the side of the road crying. I can't tell you the pain and embarrassment I felt at that moment. I couldn't tell if I was more embarrassed because everyone on the bus knew it was our stuff or because, moments before, I had been laughing at what was now my own disaster.

As I saw my mother standing there with tears in her eyes, yelling and screaming at the people who were trying to dig through our things, I knew then I never wanted my children to ever experience that feeling. I cried like never before, not so much for me, but for my mom. Shaking, crying, and trying to console me, she simply held me close and said, "It's going to be okay." She seemed broken. A piece of me died that day. I felt broken, battered, and abused though no one had laid a hand on me. As one thing dies, something else will be birthed in its place. That day, I made a declaration in my spirit that I would never feel that way again.

A GIFT

We all want to beat our chests and say "Look at me! Look how great I am." We all want the "likes" on social media and to feel we are the most important person in every room we enter. In a generation filled with the lure of outward acceptance and superficial relationships, humility can be hard to find. In a time where anyone can become famous for doing nothing, humility is the one characteristic we need most.

One of the greatest things my mother ever gave me was her work ethic. Every day for twenty-five years, she worked for the Department of Energy. On several occasions, she said I should also set my sights on the government. She believed this would guarantee me a job in the future. I remember the countless days she came home exhausted, yet still had enough energy to feed all of us. She always made it happen.

I knew we didn't have much, but my family always taught me to be thankful for what I did have. When I was seven, my aunt Teresa, or "T" as we call her, taught me how to groom myself. She taught me that every day I was to clean myself and put on clean clothes. She took the time to teach me how to brush my teeth and comb my hair every day. I learned how to iron and wash my own clothes by the time I was eight.

Being in the house with eight women, two bedrooms, and one bathroom, I had to be an early riser because bathroom time was limited. That pays off for me today, as I am still outnumbered in my house. My aunts, Wadija, Christal, Teresa, Cheryl, Venessa, and Sharon, all taught me something about women. Over the years, I have seen the unstoppable strength they possess. They were all equipped with a "never quit" spirit, which allows them to persevere in every situation they face. They are the queens in our family, and I am so thankful to have them in my life. I have seen them overcome all of life's trials and tribulations and keep moving on.

Although I never thought I would, I did eventually move past my anger and the broken feeling I felt that day. I'd like to say it was soon after, but it wasn't until I could care for my own daughter that I really let go.

W.O.W. #3 BE HUMBLE

"For those who make themselves great will be humbled, and those who humble themselves will be made great."

(LK 14:11)

Life has a way of humbling us and showing us what's really important. It takes strength to be humble. Humility is letting go of what we want and accepting God's best for our lives. If you want to live, you must learn to die to what you think is best for your life. Trust that the one who created you knows and wants what's best for you. I never forgot that day when our furniture was placed on the side of the road, and to this day, it keeps me humble. What keeps you humble?

CHAPTER 4

SACRIFICE

———

How can we prevent the next three generations from throwing their lives away? Sacrifice

In his poem, *Something to Live For,* Harold Green III asked, "What's more dangerous? Someone who's not afraid to die, or one who has found everything to live for?" Every day, families are being destroyed and futures are being lost because many of our fathers have failed to sacrifice to save their children. Sacrifice only comes when a person realizes the pain and suffering others may endure if they don't intentionally act on behalf of others. Having something to live for is the foundation of a life filled with hope, and hope is what a father's presence provides.

Hope is needed when life deals us a hand that we don't want but still must play. Hope always looks forward through the lens of faith. Every man must develop the sacrificial gene to change the DNA of fatherhood for the next generation. Realizing the obligation we have as men, changes the perspective of every situation and breathes optimism, patience, and joy into every outcome. We must give up ourselves for our children to gain their futures. My mother embodied the true meaning of sacrifice.

"Women are the vessels that keep the Spirit of God moving on the earth"

– K. JOYNER

The strength of women reigns supreme in my family. Other than my grandfather, women have dominated my life and been at the core of moving my family forward. They possess a love that is so authentic and unapologetic. Though they didn't possess names like Ida B. Wells, Toni Morrison, Rosa Parks, or Michelle Obama, they all have displayed the same unwavering spirit of strength and drive as those who came before them. The Spirit of God always gives life to every situation. It is unconditional and life-changing. Its presence always births something new. That spirit of love lives in the DNA of every woman in my family.

The Bible describes a woman as one clothed in strength and dignity and more precious than jewels. The love of a woman is like no other love in the world, and just like God, she will make the ultimate *sacrifice* to ensure her children and family are clothed with grace and mercy for maximum survival. Women have an innate instinct to nurture and care for others, especially their children. I saw this strength every day when I was with my mom, who sacrificed herself for our good. I remember the night she put herself in harm's way for me. She played the role of protector, provider, way maker, for all of us.

Nine years after I was born, she met my stepfather again; he just had a different name. Ten years and two months after I arrived, my mother gave birth to my brother Navin—her fourth child with three different men. This relationship followed the same pattern they all did.

- First, things were good, and my mom seemed happy. There were lots of parties and we often had to stay in our rooms when they were going on.

- Next would come financial problems and the blame always shifted to her.

- Finally, the physical abuse began.

One day after seeing my mother beaten so bad she could barely see, I thought to myself that no child should ever have to see their mother cry as much as I did. I would often try to catch her tears in my hands and place them back in her eyes. It is because of her unfailing love for me that I can even write this book today. She is and will always be the driving force assuring me there is nothing I can't accomplish if I am willing to sacrifice for it.

Not only did my mother sacrifice her physical self, but she sacrificed her mental self to see her children have a better life. Mentally, she never seemed happy. She never seemed to rest comfortably enough to really think about some of her decisions. She lived on her emotions and took us all along for the ride. It almost became a state of paranoia, never allowing herself to get too high in happiness or too low in depression. She became our rock, and we became everything for her. What I couldn't see was everything else that she was dealing with. The constant attacks of stress from her job and the pressure of having to provide everything we needed, with not enough money. She was our real-life superhero. My mother's strength kept us believing that things would one day be better.

When I was about thirteen, I realized that, subconsciously, I was living the same way. For a long time, I couldn't forgive the men who abused my mom because I didn't possess the strength or willingness. I wanted to carry the hate and anger for as long as I could because that was the only way I could feel better about not being able to stop it. Only God's Word and his love could take it away.

THE BEGINNING OF THE END

In the fall of 1983, our lives changed forever. My brother Navin, who was just four years old at the time got into my brother Bernie's seizure medication. He ingested half the bottle. We had just arrived at our new home, excited to see a gate and a yard for the first time. After touring the house as only kids can, filled with laughter and excitement, I went downstairs to the basement and found my baby brother. He began to shake uncontrollably, and his eyes rolled back into his head. As his body collapsed, I caught him before he hit the ground.

With my heart pounding in disbelief, I grabbed him and ran upstairs as fast as I could, hysterically screaming for my mom and his dad to help him. We got him to the hospital, and it was all a blur. All I know is that shortly after he arrived, the doctors worked to stabilize him. He spent a week there, and shortly after that, we moved out of the house we were once excited about. Navin, however, would stay with his father until he was well into his teens. It was hard on my mom because she never wanted to be away from him, and she fought to see him every day.

To this day, whenever I see him, my spirit jumps with joy because I know God saved his life that night. We all would have missed out on so many wonderful memories together. He has gone on to do some great things with his life. Out of the four of us, ironically, he would be the first to graduate from college. After all the difficulties he faced, his life would sour to tremendous heights. At twenty-two, he purchased his first investment property and has built a solid foundation for his family. He has also restored his relationship with his father. More importantly, he's become a great father, and that made it all worth it.

W.O.W. #4 LEARN HOW TO DIE

For if you want to save your own life, you will lose it; but if you lose your life for my sake, you will find it.

(MT 16:25)

To this day I don't know how my mother did it—how all her children made it out and beat the odds that many fell prey to. I can only hope, as I continue to parent my own daughter, that I can be half as courageous as my mom.

- A father's sacrifice means paying the full price for something that has not yet been fully developed or realized. Fathers must give up their lives to gain something worth living for. When we learn how to die to selfishness and become selfless, we ultimately gain a greater existence. What are you living for, and what are you willing to die for?

- Sacrifice always reminds us that there is something greater than ourselves. You must learn to die to what you feel, think, see, and experience to receive God's best for your life. It won't be easy, but you can do it. It simply requires putting God first in everything you do. Remember, he wants you to be successful!

MOMS

My mother did everything she could to ensure she raised us right. She taught me how to be respectful to others and how to be strong. She taught me how to work hard through her example. She developed a "never quit" spirit in me that gave me confidence in certain areas of my life, and she showed me what real love was. However, despite everything she did, she could never teach me how to be a *man*. To all my mothers, your sons and daughters need their fathers. They need to have a healthy relationship with him to fill the void of emptiness, self-esteem, and love that may be missing in their lives. It is vital that, if possible, this relationship be fully developed. One of the things that I am most grateful for was that my mom never enabled me as a young man. She instilled in me that the world didn't owe me anything and if I wanted something I had to be willing to sacrifice for it.

WITHOUT
A FATHER

FROM FEAR TO FAITH

PART II

BE YOU

"To be yourself in a world that is constantly trying to make you something else is the greatest accomplishment."

– RALPH WALDO EMERSON

No one can be you, like you. No one on earth has your exact makeup. Your eyes, fingerprints, and DNA are uniquely gifted to only you. You were designed and crafted to be an original, not a copy. But why have so many of us decided to abandon our uniqueness and settle for the mediocrity of being like someone else?

I grew up in a generation that wanted to "Be Like Mike." Once, when asked if he could fly, Michael Jordan said, "For a little while." The image he presented appealed to the masses and eventually made him a global icon. This propelled the Air Jordan brand into a billion-dollar industry. In fact, Michael has made more money from his shoe deals than he ever made playing basketball. Perception often becomes a reality for how we view ourselves and others. You might think being yourself is quite easy. In a world of filtered images, instant perfect pictures, and idolization of athletes, actors, rappers, and entertainers, it seems we are all trying to be like someone else.

As my life unfolded, I learned to be myself. It seemed, however, that I always had to learn the hard way. It became an endless maze of always changing to fit the image of others. Truthfully, I thought I knew who I was as it related to my family and surroundings. I thought I understood my place in this world. I knew, like you, what I had been told and what everyone said I was. But I had never truly understood who God said I was.

Being yourself in this world is going to be a daily battle from within, and the only way to win is to walk with God. As I entered my teenage years and beyond, life became my greatest teacher. Lessons of pain, failure, struggle, and victory have helped me find my identity, and they can help you as well.

MORE QUESTIONS THAN ANSWERS

Dr. Myles Munroe, author, and evangelist, once said life's most pressing questions are, "Who am I? Why am I here? and Where am I going?" Growing up without my father left me with more questions than answers. It left me to somehow figure out things I didn't even understand myself. You may also be feeling a sense of uncertainty and insecurity. As you begin part two of this book you will see where life began to give me answers I didn't want.

WHO AM I?

Sometimes we need a reminder to answer the question **Who am I?**

Then God said, "Let us make mankind in our image, to be like us. Let them be masters over the fish in the ocean, the birds that fly, the livestock, everything that crawls on the earth, and over the earth itself!" So God created mankind in His own image; in his own image God created them; he created them male and female.

(GEN. 1:26-27)

When I was a teacher, I trained my students to ask questions to explain difficult concepts. I told them whenever I said something or we read something together that they didn't understand, they should ask for "the breakdown."

Now you may have read this verse a million times or you may be reading it for the first time. Either way, here's the breakdown: You and I are made in the same image as the one who is all, has all, knows all, and created everything. We have been given royal authority to dominate the things of this earth. We are spiritual beings having a human experience.

Let that sink in for a minute.

WHY AM I HERE?

"You are the only problem you will ever have, and you are the only solution."

– BOB PROCTOR

My world did change, but only when I began to believe and walk with God's word in my soul. This question is connected to your purpose because everything God has made serves a purpose. In addition, everything he has created came designed with the ability needed to fulfill that purpose. Birds came with the ability to fly, and fish came with a built-in mechanism to help them swim. You and I also came here for a purpose. We are designed to be great and accomplish something greater than we can imagine. Your uniqueness is directly grafted into your purpose. Today, write your answer to this question - Why am I here?

WHERE AM I GOING?

In today's society, most people will simply use Google, Waze, or some form of GPS for directions. Where you're going in life is not so easy. What is your destiny? Early on, I was never worried about where I was going—I just knew I didn't want the life I had. Trying to escape your past won't lead you to your destiny. Where you are going is wrapped up in your purpose, and until you find that, you will always be headed in the wrong direction, so just BE YOU.

Part two of the book takes you through my journey of finding answers to all these questions.

CHAPTER 5

THE YOUNG MAN

———

Ben Franklin once said, "Most men die at age 25, but just aren't buried until age 75."

You can get more bees with honey than you can with vinegar. "Please" and "thank you" will be door openers for you. These were words of wisdom my grandmother gave me when I was younger but couldn't understand. As I got older, it seemed her words were ahead of there time but seemed to show up perfectly in my future. How could she know I would need these tools on my journey through life? Could it be she had been tested by them herself and learned what a powerful gift they were in her own success? She loved me and wanted to ensure I didn't make the same mistakes she had, so she passed her wisdom on to me. People who love you will always give you correction for the future, people who don't will watch you fail and then blame you.

DEAD THINKING

Now, I am in no way stating that those who grow up without a father are doomed to become a product of their environment, helpless in their own fate. However, the importance of the father's influence is greatly underestimated, and the impact of not having real men in place is being felt in every area of our society today. I believe most young men are dead from the neck up by age eighteen if they are not adding to their current knowledge. As a young man having gone through traumatic experiences, I believed I had the world figured out. As a result, I used what little knowledge I had to dictate how I would live out the next thirty years of my life. I didn't understand that I had to continue growing my knowledge, *because anything that's not growing is dead!*

Here's how it works:

From birth to age five, everything you know or need is given to you.

From ages five to nine you're putting the knowledge you have been given together with information from the world we live in. You begin to understand the differences between boys and girls, numbers, shapes, and sizes. You begin to use some of what you are taught in school and at home to define yourself and the world.

From ages ten to eighteen, you are forming your own identity and either strengthening or weakening your knowledge of the things you have been taught. By age eighteen, we only have about eight to ten years of solid knowledge, yet we think we know more than our parents. I had no true role models other than my grandfather, who didn't have a consistent presence in my life at this time. I had no one who looked like me to help guide and nurture me through my masculine journey.

TRAINING CAMP

Train up a child in the way he should go and when he old, he will not depart from it.

(PROV 22:6)

Tom Brady doesn't take the field without his coach, Bill Belichick. Clemson couldn't have won the National Championship without Dabo Swinney. Apple, which recently became the first trillion-dollar company, couldn't have done it without great leadership and training. We wouldn't send men into battle without intense training and expect them to be successful, would we? We all need a coach, trainer, or guide to help us navigate in the trenches of life. Why, then, do we have so many young people who lack the training they need to succeed in real life? A father's absence cripples the future of his children and the community.

In this life, you are either trained or untrained. You either know or you don't. You either have the skills to be successful or you don't. One of the greatest things I've learned is that every skill necessary for success *can be learned*. When I got my first job at McDonald's, they trained me on the breakfast and lunch menu; as a result, I could cook thirty-six hamburgers in less than twelve minutes. Today, I can still make pancakes like the ones they serve, because even though I'm older, the training never left me. In the same way, when a civilian signs up for any branch of the military, they must go through basic training. All training is designed to ensure that the trainee is both effective and productive in the role they were placed in. For much of my life, I felt like I had missed training camp.

Since I grew up without a father, there was no one to train me on how to live as a real man. I often said that growing up without my father felt like I was right-handed but my right arm was missing. As a result, I had to overcompensate in every area of my life to try to become successful. Often, it didn't work. It was much like when you were a kid and some adult would just pick you up and throw you into the pool, not even knowing if you could swim. Every child can be successful when equipped with a certain set of skills, but when you put children in the deep end of the pool of life without the training they need, they will eventually drown if we don't save them.

My mother did what hundreds of millions of single mothers have been doing since the beginning of time; she raised four children by herself and made a way for all of us to be successful. I certainly had the support and love of my family, but at age 9, I had to walk in the role of "man of the house" even though I had no training and reference point.

My teenage years were a blur of repetitive thoughts of not being good enough to be great—an idea given to me by my stepfather—but being cool enough to be average. This idea came from the streets, which were calling me. The lure of fast money, cars, and women became attractive, and it could have gone either way for me. However, my mom kept me focused—most of the time.

It was a time when Go-Go bands were just starting out, coupled with a growing epidemic of black-on-black crime fueled by the rise in popularity of the devil's newest drug, crack cocaine. Between 1979 and 1983, we constantly moved, and I lost many friends to the violence of the streets. DC was growing and, by the early '90s, would be tagged with the unpleasant honor of being the murder capital of the world. My mother was worried this violence would soon add me to the list of tragic deaths.

By the time I reached age eighteen, I had very little knowledge of my father and of myself. My experiences were cultivating a person who would never be able to trust and whose heart and mind would be closed for a very long time. My sister often said that during those years, I rarely smiled but was always strong. I felt dead on the inside, and I didn't know why. There was a void in my life that couldn't be filled by the streets, money, or even my dream of one day playing in the NBA.

OVERCOMING THE DEAD MAN

Trying to navigate in the world is difficult. Trying to navigate in the world without God is impossible. In my limited thinking, I thought I could solve all my problems by myself. I thought I had enough in me to do it alone. The only way I could overcome the empty, dead, and broken feelings in my heart and mind was by using the wisdom of those who came before me and through God's Word. It was hard to trust in God's Word initially, but once I took that first step, he has never let me down.

I tell you, you can pray for anything, and if you believe that you've received it, it will be yours.

(MK 11:24)

- **Believe** – First, God's Word will shine a light on the dark places in our lives. It will show us where we truly are and how to move forward. If you want something you have never had, you must do something you've never done. God's Word is not spiritual magic; you must believe and apply what it says to experience God's best for your life.

- *Meditate* – This simply means that you speak God's Word to yourself. You will gain strength and insight into how God thinks when you study his Word. Remember, always add to your knowledge of the one who created you. Decision-making becomes easier when God is leading you.

- *Obey* – Every time we obey God, we get a greater reward. When we obey his Word, he will teach us how to use truth in our lives. Wisdom always leads the way.

W.O.W. #5 EMBRACE WISDOM

Trust in the Lord with all your heart, and lean not on your own understanding, but in all your ways acknowledge him, and he will direct your paths.

(PROV 3:5-6)

Wisdom is the ability to use and apply correct knowledge and understanding in order to produce beneficial and productive decisions. Learn from those who have come before you. Wisdom offers us the gift of wise counsel, understanding, and power. It's like having the answers to the test before you take it. God's wisdom has no errors or flaws; it's will always move you in the right direction. Don't wish life was easier; wish you were better.

CHAPTER 6

HOOD LESSONS

———

Let life teach you - In every situation there will be an opportunity to learn and grow.

Woulda, Coulda, Shoulda. Have you ever wished you could keep all the great moments in your life and throw away the bad? I know I have. Pain, disappointment, and difficulties are all aspects of life we want to avoid.

Life is designed to provide your soul with the perfect tools, the perfect circumstances, the perfect conditions with which to realize and experience, announce and declare, fulfill, and become who you really are. (Twitter)

Growing up in some difficult neighborhoods heightened my instincts and opened a door for a wealth of knowledge to be discovered.

"Tell me and I forget, teach me and I remember, involve me and I learn."

– BEN FRANKLIN

Don't carry your past like a burden or a weight. Instead, think of it as a university of knowledge from which you gain several degrees. I picked up my first degree in some of the toughest neighborhoods in the DC metropolitan area. Some will spend their whole lives trying to make it out of the hood, but many won't. This place is like no other. It is a place we often visit but not a place anyone wants to stay. The hood disguises itself as a thief that steals hopes and dreams on a daily basis. It can cultivate a hate unprecedented in its fury. It destroys life without remorse or apology. However, if you have to stay for a while, learn all you can. While everyone else was trying to make it out, I was learning valuable lessons that would ultimately prepare me for life. Now, I don't condone fighting to solve problems, but in the hood, you must adopt a different mentality. The first and most crucial lesson was how to fight.

LEARN HOW TO FIGHT

When I was around 12, my mother would send me to the store with what little money she had to buy what we needed for the house. Before I learned to fight, I learned to run. This didn't last for long because, by the time I got home, the eggs were broken, the bread was smashed, and milk was all over the bag.

One day while on my way to the store, two guys jumped me and took all the money. "Mom," I said with tears in my eyes. "They took it. I got in a fight with two boys and they took the money," I said with my head down. As ashamed as I was that I had lost the fight, I was even more ashamed that I had to tell my mom all the money was gone with nothing to show for it. After all the yelling and screaming, she marched me and my brother and sister out to the corner and began questioning everyone in the neighborhood. How embarrassing!

Here's where I learned to fight, and probably when I fell in love with math. I learned to take different routes to the store, but even if I made it there, I knew I would have to make my way back. After getting all the groceries with the $10 my mother gave me, I would stop for some penny candy (back then, penny candy really did cost a penny). I then put all the remaining money in the bottom of my sock. Here's where math came in handy. Buying that candy helped me make change, which would be key to my trip back. Even if I met those two boys again, they would only get the little change jingling in my pockets. With each encounter with those boys, I got better. Pretty soon, I was better at fighting than I was at running.

If you can't and don't fight back in the hood, you become a victim both physically and mentally. Fighting freed me from ever becoming anyone's victim. It allowed me to channel my anger against those who were trying to harm me, but, psychologically, it freed me from all the times I wished I could have fought for my mom but couldn't. It made me see that not only could I use my strength, but I could also use my mind to navigate myself out of trouble.

The hood birthed the lion spirit in me, which caused me to become determined, disciplined, and a fighter for the small voice that lives inside us all—the voice that says, "I am somebody." If you are ever going to be successful, you must learn how to fight the giants who come up against you.

Physical fighting rarely solves any problem. It only magnifies the insecurities many people have. It is a temporary solution to an emotional situation. Now, I'm not saying there aren't times when you will have to fight, but you must learn to fight with your mind. It wasn't his physical strength Dr. Martin Luther King Jr. used to win the fight for civil rights—it was his mind. By studying the revolutionary, nonviolent practices of Gandhi, he saw a real solution to social injustice for African Americans and, eventually, all people. Like Dr. King, we must use our greatest weapon to fight in every situation we face—our minds. He accomplished mentally what couldn't be accomplished physically.

Learn to fight with your mind. The hood developed a mental strength that gave me the power to face my deepest fears. Your mental toughness will be just as important as your physical prowess. Mentally, I developed a confidence that would eventually train me on how to speak up for myself and develop a voice of strength. People with great mental strength are more likely to display positive behaviors; it doesn't make you perfect, but it does give you a tool you can use to rise above every situation you face. The greatest weapon you possess is your mind!

TRUST YOUR INSTINCTS

One night I was hanging out in the Southview Apartment complex where we lived. I didn't trust my instincts, and it almost cost me everything. The street corner was more of a home to me than my own house. I lived there in my mind as if I would forever be a part of it—crazy thinking. Being inside only reminded me how much my mother was struggling to make ends meet, and hanging on the block kept me distracted from thoughts about my dad.

It was a warm night with people hanging out in front of one of the popular apartment buildings near the middle of the complex. Music played on the boombox as the guys and girls socialized off to the side; the aroma of marijuana was thick in the air. Things seemed normal as I hung with the guys—who were much older than me. However, I looked up to them because I had no other role models.

I found myself in a dice game. It wasn't my first, but it would be my last. As the game began, I was up a couple of bucks. Everybody was chillin' until a guy came down the steps and asked if he could get in on the game. I felt good and the dice were on my side, so we all said, "Yeah, if you got money."

I had never seen him before, which was the first red flag. But his money was green just like everyone else's, so I ignored it and we rolled on. I lost that round, and he got the dice and went up against another guy in the circle. Everybody was dropping their money down with side bets in hopes of making even more money. Just before he rolled the dice, this girl who lived on the third floor walked through, and we all stopped and looked. If looks were thoughts, we'd all be in trouble because she was fine.

As the game continued, an argument broke out between this new guy and a friend of mine. When you roll dice in the hood, you better know the rules because things can get ugly when money is involved. Soon, everyone calmed down and the game started. My friend made a joke about shooting anybody who touched his money. Then it happened.

As the new guy reached over the money to pick up the dice, a gun fell out of his jacket! Like roaches when the lights come on, we all scattered out the door. While running, I heard two shots, which sounded like firecrackers on the fourth of July ringing out, only it was August. I ran so fast my heart felt like it was beating out of my chest. Real fear came over me, and I could barely catch my breath. I remember hiding under a car trying not to breathe, with my hand over my mouth to keep from being heard. I laid as still as I could, hoping this was not the night my life would end. Then in the distance, I could hear the faint sound of a police siren coming our way and the footsteps of the shooter running off in the opposite direction. I made it home that night, but I was never the same. I knew then that this wasn't the life I wanted.

Remember woulda, coulda, shoulda. If I had listened to my instincts, which translates into the "Holy Spirit," I would have left the game at the first red flag.

LISTEN TO YOUR INNER VOICE

"There is a way that seems right to a man, but its end is the way to death."

(PROV. 16:25)

In his book *Instinct*, author T. D. Jakes talks about how our instincts are connected to the inner wisdom of who we are, what we are created to accomplish, our calling, and life's plan. We are all born with innate instincts that have helped us survive from birth until now. The "fight or flight" instinct helps guide us away from the dangers of life and into the place of purpose. Your divine DNA gives you a unique insight into every situation you encounter. This inner instinct is one you can't shake and should never be ignored.

BE LOYAL

"A friend loves at all times, and a brother is born for adversity"

PROV. 17:17

Think about all the people you have met in your life who have started out as your friends but eventually betrayed you. I think the O'Jays said it best, "They smile in your face, all the time trying to take your place, those backstabbers."

What if you could have avoided some of the backstabbers? What if you had the gift to determine who would be loyal to you and who wouldn't? Well, in the hood, you must learn this lesson quick or it could lead to your demise. When I was younger, I used to talk a lot of trash. I could get you stirred up in a minute with my words. One night, my mouth wrote a check my body couldn't cash. I started running my mouth to this guy, but little did I know he had his whole crew with him.

There were three of us and at least eight of them. Even as we were outnumbered, I stepped up and, in my arrogance, said, "Man, this isn't fair. You guys have eight and we have three. You better go get some more people." We took a beating that night. One of the guys with us took off running and abandoned us. That's when I learned what loyalty truly meant.

Loyalty is defined as a strong feeling of support and allegiance. Growing up without my father, I felt abandoned a lot, and I never wanted to be around people who made me relive that pain. Betrayal cuts into the deepest part of our soul. It often leaves scars that never heal below the surface. It's a pain we must choose to let go of.

That "friend" was never allowed to hang with us again and was forever known in the hood as a coward. (Well, that's not exactly what we called him, but I won't use those words.)

A neighborhood produces a culture of loyalty and a sense of family—whether it's your local neighbors who are all part of the local Neighborhood Watch (which helps support the overall safety of everyone) or single mothers who both work and go to school who look after one another's kids between shifts. Neighborhoods create a sense of belonging and loyalty no matter what the conditions are. God's Word will help to produce truth in your life, but it's up to you to choose to walk in that truth.

KEEP YOUR WORD

In the days before credit, contracts and collateral paved the way for all of today's legal jargon—a man's word was all he had. Every man must guard his reputation and be impeccable with his word. If you say you're going to do something, you do it.

These two qualities will make you an asset to people and not a liability. Never ignore your gut. It's built to give you insight even when the situation is unfamiliar. We all want and need support. We will innately give our allegiance to people who willingly align themselves with us. This is why many of our youth join gangs. They feel the unconditional love and support, which they are not getting at home or school. We all want and need family.

The choices we make will eventually show us where our true loyalty rests. God has and will always give us his loyalty if we are obedient to him.

WORK HARD

Nothing ever comes to one, that is worth having, except as a result of hard work."

— BOOKER T. WASHINGTON

The final lesson I learned from growing up in a difficult environment was the principle of **working hard**. Now, I saw a lot of guys working hard on the corner to make a lot of money in a short period. I also noticed that either they didn't last or the money didn't last. I also saw my mom working hard every day to feed her children—never complaining or wanting to walk away from that responsibility.

Hard work at its core drives our souls to complete even the most strenuous task. Each of us, however, will define hard work differently. The broker on Wall Street has a different view of hard work than the migrant working in a third-world country. The coach of a high school football team will define hard work differently than the nurse who works the night shift at an inner-city emergency room. Hard work, however, is the one trait that separates those who succeed from those who fail or procrastinate.

"If you are willing to do only what's easy, life will be hard. But if you are willing to do what's hard, life will be easy."

– T. HARV EKER

Hard work gave me a sense of value and made me feel like my life mattered. From McDonald's to UPS, the value of working hard has always served me well. In addition to working hard, my mom always modeled the spirit of excellence. "If you are going to do it, do right and do it well," she would say.

Dr. King referenced a street sweeper in one of his speeches. He said, "Sweep streets like Michelangelo painted pictures, or like Beethoven composed music, and even like Shakespeare wrote poetry." In other words, no matter what your job is, do it and be the best at it. If you can adopt the spirit of hard work and excellence, you will be able to accomplish your goals and live your dreams. Hard work produced some of the greatest athletes in the world. Hard work builds financial security. Hard work wrote this book. If you try to avoid working hard, you are cheating yourself of one of life's greatest gifts.

W.O.W. #6 LET LIFE TEACH YOU

In every situation, there will an opportunity to learn and grow. God wants you to succeed. He often wraps our greatest blessing in life's biggest problems. He uses adversity for our advancement. He takes trouble and turns it into triumph. Everything you go through serves a purpose to help you reach your destiny. God owns time, and nothing is wasted.

CHAPTER 7

THE IGNORANT MAN

———

THE DARKNESS

"I say there is no darkness, but ignorance."

— WILLIAM SHAKESPEARE

When people called me ignorant, it almost felt like they were cursing me out. The word itself gives off a negative connotation. When I finally looked it up, I realized it simply meant lacking knowledge and understanding.

People often say, "If I knew then what I know now, I would have done things differently." For a long time, I was ignorant of the power of who I really was or what I could become. I couldn't see past my current situation. I wasn't as focused on my education as I should have been. You see, like most young men of my generation, I thought I was going to make it into the NBA and all I had to do was get to college. As a result, I didn't work as hard as I could in school to ensure I could enter college with both an academic and athletic scholarship. I thought my athletics would be enough to get me to my dreams and keep me there. I was wrong. In my senior year of high school, just before the season started, I broke my ankle in three places during a pick-up game. As my ankle shattered, so did my dreams of ever making it to the NBA. I felt so lost and discouraged because I had no backup plan. Now many would say that Plan B is to make sure that Plan A works. Sometimes life just doesn't work out that way; however, success can still be yours.

In 1988, while attending Charleston County Community College in Waldorf, Maryland, Mrs. Hill, the mother of a young lady I dated in high school, encouraged me to put in an application to UMBC. Initially, I was considering the University of Maryland College Park, which was the larger and more popular Maryland campus. However, she suggested a smaller school might be a better fit for me. She was right. Right away my fear and feelings of not being good enough kicked in, and I began to talk myself out of it.

"I think I'm going to wait until next year when my grades are better," I said. She responded by asking, "What do you have to lose? If you don't get in, then reapply next year." I had adopted an all-or-nothing philosophy, not understanding all dreams and goals take time to manifest. The very thought of filling out a college application gave me tremendous anxiety. Would I be good enough to get in? What would it be like to be away from home for the first time? I was also afraid of not being accepted. Fear has the potential to paralyze you and keep you from your destiny; *fight it and just take the first step.*

Going all in, I submitted the application, paid for it myself, and guess what—I got accepted. It was as if my family and I had won the lottery. I never dreamed I would ever go to college without playing basketball, but I believed what my family had told me—that I was special and would do something good with my life. Just before I went off to college, I celebrated with my whole family. Even before I left, I felt I had already won.

About a week before I left, my mom got a call and handed me the phone. It was my dad. It was a little awkward because we hadn't seen or talked to one another in what seemed like forever. Just before I left for school in August of 89' he stopped by the house, but he didn't come in. We stood outside in the driveway near the trunk of my mom's car. We settled on a little small talk about how I felt and what I thought I wanted to major in at school. However, there still a distance between us and the conversation quickly dried up. There was a long pause, then he looked at me as if to say, "I'm sorry I wasn't there for you." I looked back to say, "I hope I can make you proud", but neither of us could voice what we were feeling.

How do you restore a relationship that had been buried for years and was covered with so much resentment? I didn't know and neither did he, so we left it there; still broken. We didn't talk for long, but what he said began to shine some light on the darkness in my life. He reintroduced me to Christ, and said: *"The closer you are to God, the closer you will be to accomplishing your goals and dreams, but the further you are from him, the further you will be from discovering who you really are."*

With limited knowledge of my father, like most young men, I found it hard to trust in the wisdom he provided because I didn't know if he really cared about me. Therefore, it went in one ear and out the other. Part of me wanted badly to cling to every word he said, but pride had already taken root in my soul. There were so many things I lacked and didn't know about being a man, that it kept me living in darkness for the first twenty-five years of my life. I don't want you to think that it was all him. I made some decisions on my own that kept me from discovering what God had for me.

THE LIGHT TURNS ON

Students:

Nothing shines the light on darkness like knowledge, truth, and understanding. The weapon you can use to strike back at a world that may be trying to knock you down is knowledge. When I got to college, I was blessed to encounter Professor Lynch. I had never met anyone quite like him. He embodied our culture and was a wealth of knowledge. I remember most that he always talked about how much he loved his children and how proud of them he was. He taught African American Studies in a way no one could. We started with *The Autobiography of Malcolm X*, and from that moment, the light switch was on. I realized that when it came to my education, I had floated through high school under the dim light of what I was truly capable of, but now *the light was on in my soul for knowledge.*

- **Knowledge** – The history of African Americans is slanted, to say least, in every textbook in America. None of them truly tell the history of who we are and what we have done to build, develop, and change this world. The knowledge of who we were and what we've done in history made me see myself differently for the first time. It's vital *that every person know and understand their history* and that it is constantly passed down to each generation. Knowledge empowers and transforms the weak into the strong, the follower into the leader. What I love about knowledge is that it can be used by all, no matter your race, ethnicity, or socioeconomic status; knowledge is the great equalizer.

Teachers:

While curriculum, lesson plans, and test scores are all important, the most crucial aspect of teaching remains developing a sincere and intentional relationship with every student. Your classroom is the safe space that every student needs to rise to his or her greatest level of achievement. It must be a place that not only makes them feel comfortable but where they experience connection and appreciation of who they are. I knew going into the classroom that I had to connect academically, socially, and emotionally with all my students, but one thing that made my classrooms thrive was being able to connect culturally with everyone.

I knew being culturally responsible would make a difference in the lives of the children I was leading just as Professor Lynch had made a difference in my life. We often skip over culture and race in the classroom. It's taboo for some, just like talking about God. Ironically, I've rarely met a teacher who doesn't pray. Do you take the time to learn and relate to the students that have been placed in your care? It's not enough to know where a child comes from or what they may be dealing with; we've got to process how all of this affects their overall learning and behavior. We've got to go deep if we are going to elevate every child. This one revelation took my teaching to another level.

Geneva Gay, a prominent author in the field of culturally responsive teaching, defines it as "using the cultural characteristics, experiences, and perspectives of ethnically diverse students as conduits for teaching them more effectively."

- **Truth** – We take for granted what we don't value. It used to be a law to keep people who looked like me from learning how to read and write. When I read some of the old laws enacted by states like North and South Carolina, it gave me a sense of urgency and responsibility to do more with the opportunity I had. History had afforded me hope that wasn't always available. When I became a teacher, I never let my students forget that their education would make them unstoppable. I believe everyone must know the history of the oppressed to gain perspective and a true understanding of how history dictates some of our present conditions.

- **Understanding** – Proverbs 4:7 says that to start being wise, you must first get wisdom. No matter what it costs, get understanding. Gaining a true understanding through education gave me a greater feeling of self-worth and made me ambitious to learn even more.

W.O.W. LEARN TO LOVE KNOWLEDGE;

Knowledge is the power that makes you a superhero. It is the tool that shines the light on right decision-making. Its insight digs through the darkness of our lives and illuminates the best and most prosperous path for us all. Having an under-standing of what you may face or are going through brings an awareness that gives you the power to navigate successfully through life. People used to say that ignorance is bliss. No! Ignorance is poverty, deferred dreams, stolen destiny, and a life filled with devastating regret. Learn all you can!

As you think, so you are. As you are, so you act"

- JAMES ALLEN

CHAPTER 8

FRIENDSHIP

———

"Friendship is the hardest thing in the world to explain. It's not something you learn in school. But if you haven't learned the meaning of friendship, you really haven't learned anything."

— MUHAMMAD ALI

Letting people into my heart or even my circle was always difficult for me. I never trusted anyone except my siblings and close family. Simply put, I never wanted to give anyone the opportunity to hurt me, so I built a wall emotionally and socially. It was a wall that took years for me to tear down because I really wanted a friendship with my dad. As I said before, an absent father affects every aspect of a child's development.

In this life, it all comes down to choices. We don't get to choose our family, but we do get to choose our friends. During this season of my life, that voice in my head told me I would never amount to anything, and it grew louder each day. At the beginning of my freshman year of high school, I was headed to Central High School, located in Capitol Heights, Maryland. My mom was so nervous because she knew I was getting older and the streets were calling. I was getting into more trouble, and the people she often saw me with really had, as my mother would say, "nothing on their minds." My trust issues became worse. Whenever my mom got extremely nervous about our safety, I knew what was coming next. Yep, you guessed it. We were moving.

Unlike today's generals who often sit in a command center and give orders for the troops to carry out during a war, my mother was on the front line every day with us. She knew what we all were dealing with, and she used moving as her strategic defense to ensure our safety. So, without warning, and just a few months into the school year, I was headed to the second of three high schools I would attend before graduating. As I said before, I hated moving, but sometimes you can't see what's best for you.

My mom moved us so far away from the city I couldn't even take the bus to get back. So there I was starting over again—the new kid on the block. We moved to one of the smallest towns in Maryland at the time, Waldorf. I had never heard of it before we moved there. Initially, I hated it. There was nothing to do and no place to go and truly hangout. I was way out of my comfort zone.

My mom had met another man named Arnold, and, together, they had planned out our future. We moved for the first time to a house. I couldn't believe it. We had our own rooms, a basement, and, for the first time, green grass. We had our own lawn. This was huge for us because we finally felt we were winning, but it was just that—a feeling.

I had no real connection with my mom's new man, and he knew it. He could never replace my father nor could he win me over with gifts and this new life he was offering. Nothing and no one could ever fill the void in my life except having a real relationship with my father. It wasn't until later in life that I realized what a great man he was. He never abused my mom and only tried to make her happy. As the years went on, I could see that. Unfortunately, I never really thanked him or told him how much I appreciated him stepping in and being a provider and protector of children that weren't his own. It takes a special kind of man to have the willingness to stand in the gap for another man's absence.

I knew it was going to be difficult on the first day of school. La Plata High School was so far out that I fell asleep twice on the bus ride. When I got there, it seemed bigger than life. It a typical first day, with everyone gathering around to show off their new clothes and fresh haircuts while sharing their summer activities. There I was, holding the wall up in the corner, lost, yet trying not to look it, waiting for the bell to ring. And then it happened. I bumped into another guy, a junior, and he called me the one word that still bothers me today — the N word. That made me angry, and I hit him so hard I thought I broke my hand. This is when I first learned I had to accept the consequences for my actions. The principal said because it was the first day, he wouldn't suspend us if we shook hands and apologized to each other.

My mom had one rule—if she had to leave work to come to the school for discipline, there would be major trouble. Even though by this time I was stronger and taller than my mom, she wouldn't hesitate to go upside my head. While sitting there, I debated the consequences, but this time it was about my character. I never wanted anyone to call me that word, no matter what race they were. You probably already deduced that I didn't shake his hand, and I took an earful from my mom, but it was worth it. You see, I didn't often forgive in this season of my life. I simply didn't have the capacity.

My ninth-grade year was a blur. If it wasn't for basketball, I wouldn't have so easily made the adjustment. Sports was always my way in. It helped me in the hood, and it helped me in this new suburban lifestyle. I used it to block out all the pain

I had endured in my life. It also made me socially acceptable even in times when I wasn't confident in myself. There I was, a freshman playing and working out with the varsity team in my first year of high school. Now I was still learning the game, but it felt good being out there. However, just as I was coming into my own, it happened again. Say it with me—we moved.

You might be thinking, *Wow, again*? Yes, but what I didn't know is all this moving would eventually serve me well later in life. Ironically, we moved to an area where I got to play for the school I would eventually graduate from, Thomas Stone High School. We moved to our second home with grass and even a driveway. This was another suburban community called Pinefield. This was not the hood; it seemed like a real neighborhood, something I hadn't experienced before.

Entering this school was a little different because reputation follows you. When my coach, Steve Datcher, heard I had played at the rival school, La Plata, he immediately started watching me. I was ready to join the team, but he made it clear it wouldn't be easy. He made me work harder than ever before.

One day I met some guys from the neighborhood, and when basketball was introduced, I fit right in. I had made a lot of friends in my first year in the neighborhood, but when the dust settled, it came down to three: Mike, Sean, and Derrick. At that point, if you saw one of us you saw all of us.

These friendships were crucial at the time because these guys helped me keep dreaming and growing. They never tried to put me down or cast me out. They were faithful and true. We partied together and fought alongside one another. It was as if destiny choose us all. We grew together over the years. From girls to graduation, we made it. We even, at one time, all worked together at McDonald's. They kept me out of trouble, for the most part. We all had different personalities, but unlike some of my other friends, these guys all had good hearts. Mike was the first one of us to have a car, and back then, that was a big deal. We all piled into the Volkswagen Bug and went everywhere. If there was a football game or a party, we were there together.

These guys kept me dreaming. We used to sit around and talk about how rich we would all be, thinking money could solve all our worries. They weren't looking to cause trouble, just to have fun and be successful. Now, we did get into some trouble from time to time, but we always stayed true to one another.

STOP RUNNING

I knew something was missing in my life, but I could figure out what it was. Sometimes God has to back you into a corner for you to stop running. I grew up in the church, but as I got older, I made choices that led me further and further away from the one person who had always been there for me; God.

At age 21, I remember going to church with the young lady I was dating. Pastor Cherry preached a sermon that woke something up in my spirit. Like most people when the pastor gives the invitation to give your life to Christ, I would just stand there and look around to see who was going to move first, knowing 100 percent it wasn't going to be me. But this time was different. I slowly moved to the right, stepped out, and walked, with fear in my heart and uncertainty in my mind, down the aisle.

"What are you doing?" I asked myself. "You have no idea who God really is or even if he is real." Pastor Cherry prayed and then they took us to this room to the right of the church and talked to us about a new life in Christ. They explained that I was a new person—born again. I didn't understand it all but felt I was moving in a new direction. I had an awareness I didn't have before. Over time, as I was off to college, I lost touch with that church, but the seed had been planted and I began to want a different life.

Now, I'd like to tell you that as soon as I got saved and went off to college, everything changed in my life and I stayed on the path of righteousness from that day forward. Well, that's not my story. You see, I was running from something, but I didn't know what it was. I simply didn't think, with all the terrible things I had endured up until this point, I could be accepted by God or even loved by him.

College shines a light on your areas of weakness, and it often develops those areas and grows in a way that only difficult times and struggle can. I was weak in the area of women, and college exposed me. Being on my own allowed everything within me to come out. I had the full college experience. I partied until 4 a.m. yet still made it to my 8 a.m. classes. I stayed up late on the phone and studied just before the test. We laughed and had so much fun. Then, like a thief in the night, things got serious for me. At the same time I was discovering my gift to connect with people, I was surrounded by my weakness for women and a strong desire for pleasure. This was not a good combination.

The Bible says in James 1:14-15: "Temptation comes from our own desires, which entice us and drag us away. These desires give birth to sinful actions. And when sin is allowed to grow, it gives birth to death."

I was about to die, but it didn't involve my physical death. Instead, it involved me shedding the immaturity and insecurity of who I was. I allowed my desire to put me in a mindset of constant destruction. There I was, trying to be accepted, cool, and my own definition of what a man was, but little did I know that with every act of sexual immorality, I was killing myself slowly on the inside. Sex on a college campus seemed to be the norm. I simply fell into the pit that was waiting for me. With each act, I became less and less attached. It seemed

I was in the moment, but I really wasn't. My great-grand-mother used to say, "God takes care of fools and babies." Well, I wasn't a baby at this point. However, I was living a foolish lifestyle with very little regard for my future.

Kings: God created sex for our pleasure; however, he set boundaries for our protection. When we go outside of those boundaries, we enter into sexual immorality. Having sex doesn't make you a man. You are not a man because you have two or three girlfriends. You are not a man when you have no commitment or discipline. You are simply a male living below your full potential. Manhood and masculinity can't be given; it must be embodied. Many things will try to derail your purpose, but none is greater than the lust for women. My father didn't teach that, but God did.

Let there be no sexual immorality, impurity, or greed among you. Such sins have no place among God's people.

(EPHESIANS 5:3)

Queens: Don't give yourself over to any man who is not your husband. It may seem like a long time to wait, but you will save yourself a tremendous amount of heartache and heartbreak. When my daughter was eighteen, her heart was broken, but we were there to help her through it. I told her people will break your heart, but they may not return the pieces. Not having your father in your life may cause you to try to fill a void that can only be filled by God, and the man he has for you.

Be patient, because God knows you are a gift to him and worth waiting for.

Run from sexual sin! No other sin so clearly affects the body as this one does. For sexual immorality is a sin against your own body. Don't you realize that your body is the temple of the Holy Spirit, who lives in you and was given to you by God? You do not belong to yourself, for God bought you with a high price. So you must honor God with your body.

(1 COR. 6:18-20)

REAL FRIENDSHIP – UNBREAKABLE

One day, I guess God had had enough too, and I met the first of three people who would change my life forever. While on the court, using my gift to talk trash to everyone on the opposite team, an argument got heated and we almost came to blows. Remember, I would never back down from a fight. With odds in favor of my opponent, like a ram in a bush, God sent me a 6'1 180 lb. blessing. He stepped in and said, "I got your back," and from that day on, we would always be connected. Rohan or Ron, a.k.a. "Smoke," came to my rescue, which made me talk even more trash.

We were both from the same area, PG County, and that was all it took back then to connect us. After hanging out for a year, we eventually became roommates. I can't even tell you how much fun and laughs we shared during our college years. It was amazing.

In 1992, I met the second person who would move my life in an unexpected direction: Larry or L, a.k.a. "Boogie" and now Pastor. One day while out in the campus yard, this guy walked up in a suede vest with no sleeves. He passed out his business card and said he was a barber. Now, at that time, our campus was extremely small, and a good barber was hard to find. I had to go home just to get a haircut, so we decided to check him out.

From the first haircut, it was clear he had a gift. As the three of us began to hang out more, it was clear Larry was committed to Christ like no one I had ever seen. I had never experienced a person my age who had the fire for Christ similar to my great-grandmother. He was serious. Most importantly, he was living it out every day. After we had known each other for about six months, he called us out in the yard late one night. We sat at a small round table, and then he threw out a challenge to me and Ron.

He said, "My life is about to go in a different direction, and if you two don't come to Christ for real, we can no longer be friends."

Who does this guy think he is? I remember thinking. We had just met. No one had ever challenged a friendship in that way. He talked about all of us one day being married and our kids playing together. Really? We walked away with a lot on our minds.

You see, Larry was about to start a Bible study group on campus called FOCUS. We decided to walk with him, but on the day the Bible study was set to start, I got into a fight on the court. With my lip swollen, we still went to the first meeting, and sitting across from me was the guy I had fought earlier. I told you it was a small campus. I was the last one to really commit my life to Christ. It was a struggle, but both Larry and Ron were patient with me.

Over the years, Larry would start his journey of becoming a business owner and a pastor, and he took us both along for the ride. He modeled Christ in a way I had never seen before from someone my age. I kept waiting for him to change or slip and do something that would make him more like me; it never happened. His example helped pull me out of the world's grasp and into the light and life God wanted for me. Everything he learned, he gave to us freely in advice and wisdom.

Ron, who has always been like my big brother even though I'm older, gave me so much support and love that it was impossible for anything to ever come between us. However, one time I did stop speaking to him for about two weeks. You see, my wife—girlfriend at the time—used to make me a marble cake to take back to school after the weekend. One day after class, I had my mind set on the last piece of cake. When I got to the apartment, Ron was there. As I pulled the last piece of cake out, he asked if he could have a piece. I laughed him off. Then he did the unthinkable—he knocked the last piece of cake out of my hand and onto the floor. Now the five-second rule was still in effect, but I was so angry that we almost got into a fight. Today, twenty-seven years later, we laugh about it.

Over the years, all of Larry's words manifested. We all attended each other's weddings, and we were there for the birth of each other's children. We've helped each other move, something you know I didn't enjoy, and we've seen each other through the loss of family members, including both of their fathers. Our bond has changed the trajectory of my life and allowed me to live out my true purpose. They both encouraged me to write this book. Friendship will be crucial to your overall success. Choose wisely.

W.O.W. #8 FRIENDS EQUAL FUTURE

Your friends will ultimately determine your future, and you must choose them wisely. Your friends can change your destiny. They can alter the plan that God has for you if you allow them to. I'm not saying they can keep you from your destiny, but they can certainly put you on the wrong path. The people we choose to align ourselves with will ultimately shape our future. In the end, the only things that really matters are the family and friends we have impacted and who have impacted us. These lasting memories, which are permanently stained in our hearts, will be the greatest treasure we possess in our final days. Six people in seven years would eventually change the course of my life.

CHAPTER 9

LOVE

—

*"The best and most beautiful things in the world can not be
seen or even heard, but must be felt with the heart"*

— HELEN KELLER

Love is one of the most powerful words given to us by God. In
fact, the Bible says that God is love. Looking back over my life,
I saw that, as a result of all the brokenness, shame, and bitterness I had toward my father during my early years, I never
developed a real love for myself. You can't give what you don't
possess. I thought I knew what love was, and then I met an
angel who showed me what unconditional love really felt like.

They say you know you're in love when you can't sleep
because your reality is better than your dreams. My wife

of twenty-three years has made my reality so much better than any dream I have ever had. I never knew what real love was until I met her. When we met in 1992, I was less than a year removed from one of the toughest break-ups I had ever endured. The girl I thought I would marry simply showed up one day as I returned from college and said, "I think I need some space."

Well, back in the day that really meant, "I need some space away *from you*." It truly broke my heart. I never wanted to give someone else that kind of control over my emotions again, so for almost a year, I rested. I kept my heart protected with an ironclad wall around it. I was determined never to let anyone get that close to me again. At least that was the plan.

In the fall of '92, while on the campus of UMBC, my best friend, Ron, and I decided it was too nice to have class inside, so we didn't go. We decided to hang out in the courtyard just to sightsee until it was time for dinner. Then it happened. Amid hundreds of people, I spotted a diamond. She was simply the most beautiful person I had ever seen, and I said to my friend, "That's the woman I'm going to marry."

"Yeah, right," he said.

"No, really," I replied.

He simply shook his head and said, "Okay, but are we still going to the party tonight?"

We laughed, but the seed had been planted. Later that day, with a little investigating, we determined who her roommate was and quickly set up a time for the introduction. I remember approaching her with my same cool vibe, not feeling pressed, but giving off an air of confidence. I said, "I just want to get to know you." We spent the entire day together, and it was like we had known each other all our lives. I couldn't believe it.

At the end of the day, I walked her to her apartment, and we smiled at each other with silly, child-like passion. I shook her hand and got her phone number. From that day on, it seemed nothing else mattered. Everywhere she was, I wanted to be; everything she said, I wanted to hear.

In early December, just a few months after we were dating, we got caught up on the phone talking about her plans for Christmas break. I wanted to go to New York to be with her, but I didn't want her to feel like I was a stalker, even though since that first day in September, we had seen or talked to each other every day. I even missed my calculus class clinging to every word she said.

FALLING IN LOVE

"I fell in love like you would fall asleep, slowly, then all at once"

– JOHN GREEN

Falling in love, just sneaks up on you and often catches you off guard. It's like a tsunami that has the power to wash away all the hurt and pain we've ever been through. Its power can change minds and hearts in the blink of an eye. It gives us the boldness to face every situation head-on and makes us feel like anything is possible. It was in this space that we found ourselves slipping deeper and deeper into the magical web in which love entangles us all. What I remember most about this feeling, was that there was nothing I could do to stop it, and the truth was, I didn't want to. For the first time, my soul felt alive, and I knew I had entered something special and different.

It really got serious when one day my friends asked if I was going to play ball and I said, "I can't. I've got to see Nicole."

The barrage of jokes about me being pressed and whipped came my way, but I didn't care. I was happy to take it all on for her. Now, as the courtship progressed, I was watering the seed that had been planted just a few months earlier, both in my heart and mind. One night after about four months of stopping at the door, she invited me in to watch a movie.

I didn't want the guys to know, but we watched *Beauty and the Beast,* the original version.

I guess it appealed to me because it's a love story. I saw myself as the unrefined beast, and she was the most beautiful person I had ever met. She was one of the first women to show me real, unconditional love.

I had been with many women, some to help boost my ego. It seemed that with others, there was always some hidden agenda of status or psychological void I was trying to fill, but Nicole was different. She had a heart bigger than life, and she treated everyone with respect. I often told her she trusted people too much, but she would say, "You don't trust people enough." Who was this woman? Did God just create her for me? Yes, He did!

In every relationship I had ever been in, I always found a way to mess it up or I gave it only enough to keep it going. I had never gone all in, but this was different. I could see and feel the piece of me that was missing every time I looked at her. One of the greatest feelings you will ever experience is the unbridled joy of falling in love. The euphoria it brings to the heart breathes life into every situation.

"You know you're in love when you can't sleep, because your reality is better than your dreams"

We spent every day together talking about our hopes and dreams and walking everywhere we could. With every moment we spent together, another brick would fall from that wall around my heart until, one day, I realized I was falling in love with this woman. It was a love so powerful that it scared me. I felt so strongly about her that nothing else mattered. In this season of life, I decided to go all in not just for her, but for God

God has, is, and will go all in when it comes to his love for us. He will never leave us or forget about us. God can't love us any less than he does. His love is forever and will never fade. I often felt like my father forgot about me, and that made me feel less of a man. And when a man doesn't value who he is, he won't be able to give his all to someone else.

PATIENCE

One of the fruits of the spirit mentioned in Galatians 5:22 is patience—something I didn't have a lot of when I was younger. I wanted everything when I wanted it. My wife taught me patience.

Every day, I would leave my Chesapeake Hall dorm room at the bottom of the hill and walk to the on-campus apartments to see her. She never let me stay the night, although I tried. I learned that when something or someone is valuable, you will wait as long as it takes. She also showed patience in that she gave me time to find myself and discover my purpose.

Coupled with patience is a companion called hope. As the Bible says, hope does not disappoint.

When we met, I felt like my wife already had her wings to fly. Over the years, when money was low and I couldn't provide, when I had no direction and no focus, she was patient. I always felt like she was a butterfly and I was just a struggling caterpillar. Now, the process of metamorphosis normally takes approximately twenty-one days; mine, however, would take about twenty years. Through it all, she was there encouraging me and waiting patiently until I got my wings. Now we fly together in love in any direction we choose.

DON'T KEEP SCORE

Real love doesn't keep score. In most of my relationships, before I met my wife, I kept score. I held on to the wrongs and disappointments as though they were trophies, and I used them as pawns to manipulate and gain the upper hand. I hated it when women brought up my past and used it against me, but when it suited me, I used this weapon myself.

Through marriage, I learned I can't love my wife that way or I would fall short each day. I had to love her the way God loves her, and that meant learning how to die to myself and live for her. Over the years, I had learned to argue with the best of them, but this would never work in a marriage.

NEVER GIVE UP

"It's not the lack of love, but the lack of friendships that make unhappy marriages,"

– FRIEDRICH NIETZSCHE

Many marriages end when the friendship dies. In 2006, our love was dying, and we didn't even know if we wanted to be married. We had emotionally, physically, and psychologically checked out of the friendship, which threatened to end the marriage.

Earlier that year, I had planned a surprise party for my wife's thirty-eighth birthday. A few weeks before her birthday in July, we found ourselves so far apart that I thought it was over for us. Even though we were not even speaking, I decided to keep my word and go ahead with the surprise party. Just hours before the celebration, I saw her in a new dress with an unbelievable new hairdo. Trying to pretend I didn't notice, I let my ego get in the way and walked right by her without saying a word. None of our family or friends knew the devastation our marriage was suffering, but we did. Barely speaking, we played the charade for everyone who attended.

That night, after everything was over, I saw her for the first time like I had never seen her before. I saw her smiling and laughing, and I remembered the person I had fallen for years ago. I almost gave up on us, but I am so glad that God doesn't give up on us. God has a way of interrupting our lives to remind us of his love for us. That night, we spoke with her mom and dad and found out her mom had been diagnosed with breast cancer. For as long as I can remember, my wife has feared getting cancer because it runs in her family.

If you've ever been punched in the stomach and had the wind knocked out of you, this felt ten times worse. We couldn't believe it. Over time, our focus shifted, and we both began to see that life was more important than the battles we were fighting with one another. I only wanted to give her love and never see her cry again. It reminded me of seeing my mother cry because of my stepfather, and I only wanted her to experience joy. In the past twenty-five years, God has matured me as a husband, and through failure and his Word, I've been a better man for my wife. I am so thankful that God didn't give up on me while I was going through the process.

Psalm 23:4 says, "Yea, though I walk through the valley of the shadow of death, I will fear no evil; For You are with me; Your rod and Your staff, they comfort me. Even when we are in the darkest times in life you and I can trust that God will never give up on us. There is no place that we can go where God cannot rescue us."

ENDURANCE

Endurance means the ability to withstand hardship and adversity, and real love will always have endurance attached to it. It cannot stand in its own power. You've probably heard the saying "The race is not given to the swift, but to the one who endures until the end," and thought it came from the Bible. The first part does come from Ecclesiastes 9:11, but the second part comes from a line in Aesop's Fable, the *Tortoise and the Hare*. Both provide value to our lives and to our marriages. The verse actually reads, "I have seen something else under the sun: The race is not to the swift or the battle to the strong, nor does food come to the wise or wealth to the brilliant or favor to the learned; but time and chance happen to them all."

Nothing can prevent trouble, but if we endure, we will gain wisdom and assurance as we travel through this divine journey of faith. Real love is packed with endurance. As a result of our love, I could now go into the next half of my life equipped with the one piece of the puzzle that was missing because of my father—LOVE.

W.O.W. #9 LOVE BEYOND YOUR PAIN

God has, is, and will go all in when it comes to his love for us. He will never leave us or forget about us. God can't love us any less than he does. His love is forever and will never fade.

I often felt like my father forgot about me, and that made me feel less of a man. And when a man doesn't value who he is, he won't be able to give his all to someone else.

Love is patient and kind. Love is not jealous or boastful or proud or rude. It does not demand its own way. It is not irritable, and it keeps no record of being mistreated. It does not rejoice about injustice but rejoices whenever the truth wins out. Love never gives up, never loses faith, is always hopeful, and endures through every circumstance.

(1 COR 13:4-7)

CHAPTER 10

48 NICKELS

"Change your thinking and you will change your life"

TOXIC MENTALITY

If you want to destroy any particular people, all you have to do is take hope from them. Poverty erodes the soul and causes the spirit to live in hopelessness. It is an abuser of epic proportions. It doesn't discriminate against race, religion, ethnicity, or culture. It is a cancer that eats at the consciousness of its victims and kills the dreams and futures of so many people. Poverty shrinks the scope of possibility and develops a mindset of limited self-worth. I should know; it made me think, act, and feel that I had no value.

As I entered my thirties, I realized the poverty mindset was having a rippling effect on my life. It showed itself in the habits of my financial choices every day. Sadly, I didn't possess the skills or knowledge at that time to change it. In early 2000, I was finally working a steady job as a supervisor at UPS and making good money, or so I thought. More importantly, the benefits were great, which helped me take care of my wife and daughter. However, what hadn't changed was my knowledge of what to do with the money I was making. It showed itself in one of the most humiliating moments of my life.

One day, while headed to work *late*, not far from our apartment in Glen Burnie, Maryland, my gas light was shining brighter than the sun. I thought, *You can make it to work*, but I didn't want to take any chances. As I pulled into the gas station, I did what I always do—I called to check the balance in my account. Seventy-six cents.

As I scrambled to look under the seats of our Toyota Corolla, which had well over 100,000 miles on it, I felt nothing but pennies and nickels. I checked the ashtray, and it was loaded with more nickels. Frustrated and desperate, I gathered up as many nickels as I could, too embarrassed to take the pennies.

As I got out of the car, I pulled the hood of my UPS hoodie over my head, hoping no one would recognize me. I desperately tried to time it just right so no one else was in the store.

As I waited as patiently as I could for others to leave, I knew I was running out of time with each minute, making me later and later for work. As soon as I walked in, like a scene from that *Flintstones* episode where every line he's in gets longer, a flood of people walked in at the same time I did.

With four or five people behind me and my hands full of nickels, I moved to the counter with my head down and a heaviness in my step. After taking a deep breath, I moved toward the counter. I looked up and caught the eye of the attendant through the glass shield, and, in shame and embarrassment, I dumped all forty-eight nickels on the counter. Crazy, right?

The rush of the coins rang out like a siren, and the people behind me are like, "Really?" But it was the look on the guy's face behind the glass that brought complete humiliation. He looked at me as if to say, "What a pity." I can't even tell you what the attendant said because as soon as I released the coins, I said, "Put it all on pump two" and walked out. I felt like less than a man. As I drove to work that day, I knew I never wanted to feel like that again. Although it never got that bad again, I still had days when I had more problems than money. We get our habits about money from what see and experience growing up. I saw a lot of stress and lack in the area of finances, so I adopted these painful habits later in life. Managing money difficult mainly because I wasn't saving anything; I simply paid bills and spent the rest.

YOU DON'T KNOW WHAT YOU DON'T KNOW

Jim Rohn states that there are two challenges in life, *"the development of our full potential, the wise use of all our resources."*

I never had conversations with my mom or anyone in my early years about saving money or what to do with it when I got it. I simply did what I thought I should, never thinking about the future.

According to the National Center for Children in Poverty, there are 34,879,935 children in the US under the age of nine. Nearly 20 percent of them live in poverty. Children who live in poverty are more likely to experience social, emotional, and behavior problems. In addition, it may also impede their ability to develop and learn. These children are also more likely to experience poverty themselves as adults.

I was never taught how to save or the value of investing. When you don't know what to do with your resources, you will always pay a price greater than what you can see. Someone once said to me, "Money doesn't just behave; you have to tell it what to do." I have never forgotten that statement. Money is a tool, but if you are not intentional about how to use it, it will ultimately leave you. Most people who have amassed a great deal of wealth didn't set out to do so. Their first goal was simply to be the best or to create something new and different. This was the case for Steve Jobs, founder of Apple, and for Marc Benioff, founder of Salesforce. Both simply wanted to do something that hadn't been done before. Focus on purpose and money will follow.

The formula for making money in this country hasn't changed in over one hundred years. Make yourself valuable, meet other's needs, and bring value and consistency to the marketplace.

The Bible is a great resource for saving money. The Bible's philosophy says first to give, then to save, then to spend. This was contradicted how I lived. My philosophy was spend, spend, spend.

- **Give** – Luke 6:38: "Give, and it will be given to you. A good measure, pressed down, shaken together and running over, will be poured into your lap. For with the measure you use, it will be measured to you." Giving is good for the soul. It creates better health and develops a selfless mindset. Give 10 percent of what you gain back to God. God doesn't need our money; it's more about honor and trust.

- **Save** – Proverbs 21:20- The wise have wealth and luxury but fools spend whatever they get.

  Saving is an investment in your future and the future of those who will follow you. It is an opportunity to affect a future that you may never see. Save at least 10 percent of every dollar you earn.

- **Invest** – Ecclesiastes 11:6: "Sow your seed in the morning, and at evening let your hands not be idle, for you do not know which will succeed, whether this or that, or whether both will do equally well." We reap what we sow. Invest in something other than material possessions. Invest at least 10 percent of your income in something that can outlive you. After managing the first 30 percent of each dollar based on godly principles, use the other 70 to meet your basic needs.

When you hear the word "inheritance" what do you think of? Most people think about being left with a great deal of money by a family member. Initially, an inheritance was left for the provision and status of the family. In other words, one generation passes on its wealth, knowledge and acquired possessions to the next generation. Fathers have the task of ensuring that they leave an inheritance for their families. Growing up without my father, I didn't inherit any of these things from him. I longed for his presence, but I needed his love and wisdom even more.

W.O.W. #10 DON'T WORSHIP MONEY

Worship is made for only one person – God

Purpose is greater than money. Money must be used for its intended purpose; only then will you be able to master all your money problems.

PART III

CHANGE OF HEART

Matthew 16:25 – *For whoever desires to save his life will lose it, but whoever loses his life for My sake will find it.*

All of life and death abide in the heart. It is by far the most vital organ in the body. On average, our hearts beat 100,000 times a day and push 5,000 gallons of blood through our bodies every twenty-four hours. It is responsible for delivering oxygen and nutrient-rich blood to the tissues of our body while removing waste. The average adult heart weighs about eleven ounces and is rarely any bigger than a clenched fist. Not only does the heart regulate the flow of blood through our bodies, but it also gives us the strength for outward productivity. It is the center and governing force that controls who we are. It acts as judge and jury over our mental processes. In connection with the brain, it helps guide our decisions. It also acts as a filter and is a discerner of truth and justice. It serves as the incubator for all our emotions. This life-giving organ must be kept healthy by feeding it the one thing it needs to grow—God's Word.

When I was growing up in the Washington DC metropolitan area, there was a perception that you always had to be tough and hard, thus closing your heart to sensitivity. Weakness was seen as a dysfunction of character, quickly trampled over by those willing to do whatever it took to get some "street cred." This did nothing more than create resentment for other men and tolerance and disrespect for women in general. My heart was a cold and lonely placed filled with ambitions of greed and sexual immorality. I was misguided and untrained. It took me a long time to shake that mentality and begin to trust people I didn't know. Life had filled my heart with so much pain and hurt that I developed a sickness that had my heart completely broken. I know my heart didn't just change because I wanted it to; it took the lather of God's Word to wash away the filth and emptiness in my spirit, and that's what changed me.

LEARN HOW TO DIE

I learned how to die, and this was one of the toughest things I ever had to do. I had to die to what I believed and wanted to become what God created me to be. You can't see yourself for who you are when your thinking and vision is one-sided. I was living with a blind spot and I couldn't even see it. I was so used to doing things on my own without the guidance or input of anyone else that I often chose my own way without consulting anyone. I became my own God.

Psalm 119:9, 11 helped strengthen my inner core, which washed away the toxic thinking I had latched on to in my early days. These verses not only questioned me but gave me a clear solution. God's Word is always focused on our future. Wrapped up in it are all the things we need as we progress. The tough part was actually applying it to my life and learning how to die.

- *Psalm 119:9 – How can a young man keep his way pure? By living according to your word.* Living a great life won't be easy, but without God's Word, it will be impossible. You may even gain some level of success, but you will never gain the complete fulfillment of life without understanding and following God's Word.

- *Psalm 119:11 - Your word I have hidden in my heart, that I might not sin against you.* God's Word became a superpower in my life. It acted as a force field protecting me against all of life's troubles. Most of all, it protected me from myself. By memorizing and living out the Word of God, I was able to change my thinking and create a different outcome for my life. The words you have in your heart and believe about yourself are fuel used to push you toward your destiny or derail your purpose.

Action: Each year, I choose a word that will embody my thinking and habits and allow me to accomplish my mission of changing lives. I was first introduced to this technique when I became a teacher at Memminger Elementary School. Today, choose a word that will help you gain power and hide that word in your heart and mind. Nothing can stop the human spirit, and there is an unstoppable power in the words we speak to ourselves.

WALK HIS WAY

There is a path before each person that seems right, but it ends in death.

(PROV 14:21)

Check God's Word before you settle on a course of action for your life. Even when I think I'm right, I know God's way is always better than I can ever imagine. When I began to trust his Word and seek him for everything, I began to die to my own way of life and live with a new view perspective daily. Doubt and Fear will always make you second-guess your way, but God's design for your life is based on what is best for you and those around you. Before you start a journey, ask God to be your compass. Look up.

WORK YOUR FAITH

But do you want to know, O foolish man, that faith without works is dead?

(JAS 2:20)

Exercise your faith. The exercise equipment in the gym won't help you if you don't use it. The same holds true for your faith. If you don't use it, you will never see the power that lies in trusting in God's Word. In addition, just like the equipment, the more you use it, the stronger you become. To use it, your belief must be strong enough to move you into unstoppable action. It takes faith to drop out of Harvard University to start a company where people connect on the internet, i.e., Facebook. It takes that same faith to go from city to city selling your CD out of the back of your trunk, which has now produced a net worth of over 375 million dollars for rapper Master P. Remember, like gravity God's principles always work, but only if you exercise them.

"Be Righteous; not right – Blessed are those who keep justice, And he who does righteousness at all times!"

(PS 106:3)

For a long time, I suffered from a disease called "I'm always right." Even when I gained a different perspective from someone, I still believed my ideas were the best. I debated my point in a way that made others feel they were nothing, simply because I had to be right.

Most men equate being right with being smart. We want to be right about everything because it says we are smart and in control of the situation; it puts us on top. Often, while arguing with my wife, I knew I was right (men, you know what I mean). However, **marriage and God's Word taught me that it is better to be righteous than right.** I learned how to die to myself because I would rather be in the will of my Father then function in the will of my own flesh, which is flawed and imperfect. So that means if I am arguing with my wife—even if I am right—I am dead wrong in God's eyes. Men, save yourselves some arguments.

Over the next few seasons of life, I would have to die repeatedly to reach the destiny God had for me. These principles will help you get through the hurdles I stumbled over. Every day, it felt like a war was going on in my spirit. The war between good and evil, failure and success, and life or death was unbearable at times, but here's how I made it.

If you dare to know the truth and the importance of the role of the man in this world, then turn the page and begin your transformation. If not, stop right now because the next portion will hold your conscience accountable for the rest of your life. I dare you to turn the page

CHAPTER 11

THE NEW MAN

"Your life does not get better by chance; it gets better by change"

— JIM ROHN

Congratulations, you have just conquered one of the deepest fears most men have: We are afraid to admit we don't know and, thus, won't even try to change for fear of failure.

They say one of the greatest tricks of Satan was to convince people he wasn't real. How crazy is that? You might be saying to yourself, "I don't need God in my life" and be tempted to stop reading altogether. Don't!!

We were married just under three months before my wife gave birth. We didn't know if we were ready, but we took the leap of faith anyway. Two years prior, while sitting in a parking lot in New York waiting to see a movie, we picked out names for our son and daughter. It was important to me for us to get married before our child came into this world. You see, that was part of the cycle I was trying to break. My parents never married, and, in my mind, that had placed my life on a course filled with trauma, brutality, violence, and disappointment, all of which I didn't want for our child.

As I raced down I-95 from Baltimore to Laurel to get home to my wife, who was in labor, panic came over me like never before. What was I going to do? What kind of father would I be? Could I truly be better than the men I'd seen in my life? The one thing I knew for sure was that I wanted to be there when my child was born. You see, my father wasn't there when I was born. I wanted to be the very best father I could be for my child. Everything my father wasn't, I wanted to be.

Growing up without your father always has an effect on you; it never leaves you. You always feel like you're missing something. Many use it as fuel to push themselves so far away from the memory of their fathers that his existence gets buried in a place we rarely visit. All the hate, resentment, pain, and bitterness will produce one of two men. Most will challenge their souls to become something greater and give their children everything they lacked as a result of not having their fathers present. Others will unconsciously become *just like their fathers*. They will abandon their responsibility or abuse the mother of their children. They will become absent fathers because often you can't give what you don't have. Many men were not mentored or given the love they needed to be great men and fathers themselves. That deficit would later visit me in parenting my daughter.

When I arrived, my wife's labor pain was already at a seven on a scale of ten. I saw a look of intense pain and concern on her face. She was looking to me and needed me in a way I had never been needed before. Through the pain and tears, I saw the look of love in her eyes as if to say, "Be the man you are called be." I immediately called 911, and shortly after the ambulance arrived, I thought, *Wow, my son is on the way.* As I drove behind the ambulance headed to the hospital, I was so scared. I prayed my wife would be able to have a natural childbirth and that all would go well. Ironically, just as life always does, things turned in a different direction.

After my wife received the largest needle I have ever seen, she started having pains. The doctor said the baby was in distress and he needed to perform an emergency C-section. Scared out my mind, I asked the doctor, "What does that mean?" He said, "We've got to go now!"

They rushed us into the emergency room like a scene out of *Grey's Anatomy.* I slipped on the blue scrubs, which I still have to this day, and they rolled her in. I remember rolling through the double doors to a room on the left side of the hall. As we entered, my heart was racing both in excitement and panic. In a room filled with machines I've never seen before, the doctor and two nurses were now rushing to save the two greatest gifts God has ever given me.

I held my wife's hand as she squeezed my hand hard, and I saw a look of fear and uncertainty on her face that I had never seen before. We didn't know what we were doing, but God had already worked it out.

For some reason, I looked down and saw where they had to cut across her abdomen. I never want to see that again. In the midst of all the directions being uttered from the doctors and nurses, the machines beeping, and my heart, which felt like it was beating out of my chest, suddenly, there was silence and I heard the nurse say, "It's a girl!"

I was in total shock. What was God up to? That was the day I learned that God won't always give you what you want, but he will always give you what you need. That was the day I transformed my thinking—the day I held God's gift in my hands and became a father. Later that night as I looked at our daughter, with no money and no job, I remember looking up and saying, "God, I need your help. I can't do this without you." When you begin to live for something greater than yourself, that is the day you will be transformed.

RENEW YOUR MIND

Don't copy the behavior and customs of this world, but let God transform you into a new person by changing the way you think. Then you will learn to know God's will for you, which is good and pleasing and perfect.

(ROM 12:2)

I knew that if I wanted a different outcome for my wife and daughter, I had to change my thinking. Not having a job or money to provide made me quickly take inventory of my life. I didn't like the results. If your current situation has you frustrated, disappointed, or feeling pain or guilt, now is the time to change the way you think. One of the deadliest things a person can do to sabotage their own existence is to disregard the part of themselves which comes from the Creator.

There are indisputable truisms about who you are. The first is that, whether you are saved or unsaved, whether you believe in God or not, there are three parts to your being:

- You are a *mental* being because you can think for yourself.

- You have a *physical* presence in the body that you operate in.

- You have a *spirit* that gives life to your body.

If you fail to understand and develop your spirit, you are leaving a third of yourself out of the equation of who you truly are.

Without the governing spirit of Christ, any person is subject to eventually be controlled by their own desires, no matter how addictive or heinous they may be. To develop the whole man, the spirit man must be fully developed. Every man must build up and fortify his spiritual immune system. When we are spiritually rooted, it gives us confidence when the storms of life mount up against us. When trouble and difficult situations arise, our spiritual immune system kicks in like a force field and protects us against outside toxins.

When your spiritual superpower kicks in, sickness can't penetrate it, disappointment won't discourage you, fear can't stop you, and adversity can't move you. A man can be physically strong and mentally sharp, but if his spirit is not intact and connected to God, he could become a pedophile or rapist. Another man can be highly successful in business yet be verbally abusive to his employees and family members. To have balance and become the man you were designed to be, your spirit must be in line with God.

I often wondered why God chose Saul while he was traveling on the road to Damascus. God interrupted Saul's life and put him in a place where he couldn't see his way. Saul's unwavering and dogmatic passion to kill allowed God to transform his thinking in a way no one else could. His spirit was renewed, and soon his adversity would place him on a different path, which would make him unstoppable in his faith for Jesus. Show me a man who has developed his mind, body, and spirit and who is now using it to work fully in his God-given purpose, and I will show you a man who can't be stopped and can accomplish anything. You have nothing to lose and everything to gain; especially if doing things your way hasn't truly fulfilled your life. I've learned that very few people really want to do the work it takes to become someone new.

REAL CHANGE

"Progress is impossible without change, and those who cannot change their minds cannot change anything."

– GEORGE BERNARD SHAW

As I began my walk with God, I realized he wasn't going to force himself into my life, and he didn't want to change me. That's right. God doesn't just want to change you; he wants to transform you. The word "transform" means to make a dramatic change in form, appearance, and character. When the transformation of the butterfly is complete, nothing is left that resembles the caterpillar. Its shape, appearance, and characteristics are totally different. God wants to make you into the person he has created you to be and not what others say you should be. Knowing and growing with Him will give you your true identity.

People say practice makes perfect, but the truth is practice makes progress possible. Here are the key steps to change:

- Commit! Making a decision to commit to a different way of thinking opens the doors of our minds to new opportunities. A daily commitment that moves us toward God's desires for our lives gives us power over every situation. Your thinking, not money, status, fame, or popularity, is the number one thing that will make the difference in your life. Your mind holds the keys that will unlock your destiny. I had to learn how to exchange my thoughts for God's thoughts. We must remember that life is not happening to us, but for us.

- Honor God. Honoring God in all areas of our lives will produce a lasting change for the future. It wasn't easy for me, but I was thankful God was patient with me. He gave time to make honoring him a priority. Change doesn't come on our terms but when we make honoring God our lifestyle. Our lifestyle must line up with our decisions. For example, if we decide to lose weight, we can't keep donuts in the house. Your lifestyle must change to fit the commitment you have made for your future.

- **Ac**quire knowledge. Learning never stops, and knowledge deepens our faith and trust in God. I had to acquire a true understanding of God's Word for my life to change. My great-grandmother used to say, "You've got to know that you know, that you know, that you know." In other words, you need your own relationship and understanding of who God is to truly change. I had to put away childish thinking to develop into the man I was intended to become. Acquisition of how God thinks and moves helped me see every situation as an opportunity to gain what I needed for the next stage in my life. Ironically, the more I understood about God, the less I feared my circumstances.

- **N**ever Stop. Never stop changing your thinking in other areas of your life. Financially, eviction notices and days with no lights made me change my thinking. These moments were permanently stained in my soul and helped remind me never stop trying to improve. I had to learn to make consistency my best friend.

- **G**uard your heart. When you're trying to change, it seems like every day, distractions come at the same time, only with double the force. Proverbs 4:23 reminds us to guard our hearts, for it determines the course of life (NLT). Everything we experience must be filtered through God's Word to determine if there are any impurities that might harm our hearts and, thus, affect the course of our lives. God's Word is the protector that will guard our hearts against our desires, thoughts, emotions, and relationships. Let God's Word be the watchman that guards your heart.

- Enlarge your circle of influence. When I wanted to change, I had to seek out people who had not only traveled the road I was on but had been successful in the same area. It's hard to follow someone who hasn't walked in your shoes. God has not only walked the path we are on, but, in many instances, he has carried us. I had to leave certain people behind to upgrade and change my life.

W.O.W. #11 TRANSFORM YOUR THINKING

You must change the way you think to develop a different outcome for your life. This means that anyone who belongs to Christ has become a new person. The old life is gone; a new life has begun!

(2 COR 5:17)

When I said yes to God, it changed my outlook on life and put me on a different path. If the path you are on has you going in the wrong direction, it will be your new thoughts that will change your life forever.

CHAPTER 12

KINGS

———

I have a purpose! I was born to be great!
I will never let failure define me.

I will overcome every obstacle.
My condition will not be my conclusion.

I know that what I believe about myself, I will become.

I will be excellent in all I do. I will be successful.

— K.JOYNER

In the fall of 2015, I wrote this affirmation to remind myself of who I was. I then made it the affirmation of the non-profit I helped create, which mentors young boys. I never thought it would change my life or the lives of so many young men.

In the game of chess, the king is the most sought-after piece on the board. Destroy or enable it, and you win the game. When the king is attacked and has no way to escape, the game is over. Similarly, when the male is under attack with no escape route, his life, along with the lives of everyone he is connected to, will be affected.

The one thing that helped me grow my *faith* the most was the Bible. The stories helped make it relevant and clear how God works and what it takes to live a life that pleases him. When I first started reading the Bible, I came across the books titled First and Second Kings. I didn't know the history, but I just wanted to be a king.

One of the greatest kings in the Bible was King Solomon. Now, while king Solomon was great, he inherited his position because of his *father* David. David's initial devotion and moral commitment paved the way for his fame and fortune, which he passed on to Solomon. Once Solomon became king, he showed his greatest strength when he humbled himself.

Solomon, who was 12 years old when he became king, understood that he did not possess the knowledge or wisdom to lead the people of Israel, so he asked God for it. Not only did God give him wisdom, but he also gave him riches, wealth, and honor unlike any king before him. However, if every man is to be successful in his walk with God and his position in this world, he must remain connected to the Word of God in mind, body, and spirit.

EVERY MAN HAS A VICE, DON'T LET IT DESTROY YOU.

We know that the law is spiritual, but I am unspiritual, sold as a slave to sin.

(ROM 7:14)

THE MAKING OF A SLAVE

My first indulgence in sex was in the tenth grade. Over the next ten years, it would become my vice. By the time I was twenty-one, I had survived the trauma and difficulties with a few feathers in my cap, through grace alone. I hadn't gone through any therapy, but I just filed it all away hoping it wouldn't come back to destroy me in the end. My reckless and immoral behavior pulled me so far off the path of my destiny that I never thought God could ever use me.

I'd never had a drink, never smoked, never used drugs, and never been arrested, but I did pick up the one vice that had the potential to destroy it all: the lust for women. **Here's where we go deep.** When I hit college, I had already had sex so many times, I had lost count. Even worse was that I didn't think anything was wrong with it. College, opened the flood gates to an area of my life I had never tried to control. I neither wanted nor thought I could control the urge enough to say no. I went after whoever I wanted with a recklessness that slowly pulled me deeper into sin and away from what God wanted for my life.

Here's where the war began in my spirit. Through my sinful nature, I became a slave. Having sex out of wedlock became normal. Then I read Romans 7:14-25 in my second year of college:

So the trouble is not with the law, for it is spiritual and good. The trouble is with me, for I am all too human, a slave to sin. I don't really understand myself, for I want to do what is right, but I don't do it. Instead, I do what I hate. But if I know that what I am doing is wrong, this shows that I agree that the law is good. So I am not the one doing wrong; it is sin living in me that does it.

And I know that nothing good lives in me, that is, in my sinful nature. I want to do what is right, but I can't. I want to do what is good, but I don't. I don't want to do what is wrong, but I do it anyway. But if I do what I don't want to do, I am not really the one doing wrong; it is sin living in me that does it.

I have discovered this principle of life—that when I want to do what is right, I inevitably do what is wrong. I love God's law with all my heart. But there is another power within me that is at war with my mind. This power makes me a slave to the sin that is still within me. Oh, what a miserable person I am! Who will free me from this life that is dominated by sin and death? Thank God! The answer is in Jesus Christ our Lord. So you see how it is: In my mind, I really want to obey God's law, but because of my sinful nature I am a slave to sin.

Initially, these verses were confusing, so I never took the time to examine them in detail. Then one day while searching for something else, I came across this passage again. This time, I actually stopped to read it and let it sink into my spirit. Then it hit me: This was me! Sin was waging war against my spirit, and I couldn't do anything to stop it. My will wasn't strong enough to resist, and for a long season in my life, I was a slave. I wasn't a slave from hundreds of years ago like my ancestors, but a slave to sin, which had me mentally chained and constantly destroying myself.

LOST

Here's where I got lost. Being a male doesn't make you a man. In addition, having sex is not a true definition of manhood. Like most young men, I equated sleeping around or having several girlfriends with being a man. I thought the more women I was with, the more it defined my role as a man. **Not True!**

Real manhood is being able to control yourself in the crucial areas of your life. Sex doesn't make you a man but simply feeds the flesh. Whatever we feed grows stronger, and I was feeding it every week, if not every day. I can't tell you exactly when it happened, but when I began to obey God's Word and mature in my faith, the chains that had me bound began to loosen. I was free for the first time in my life.

The struggle to control the flesh will never leave you. Be patient and cover yourself daily in God's word.

- **Wait for it** – Many people will tell you that sex before marriage is acceptable. In a world inundated with sexual immorality, it will be hard, though not impossible, to say no. Waiting ensures a clear understanding of who you are and what you are engaging in. If you wait on God, he will give you the best experience in this area, but if you don't, you risk throwing away your future and your destiny.

- **Surround yourself** – Being single is not taboo. Surround yourself with people who can encourage you and lift you up. Don't let others pressure you into giving up your future. Surround yourself both inside and out with God's Word. It will give you strength in times of weakness. It will be hard, but it will be worth it.

YOU ARE FREE

You don't have to be a slave to sin and depravity. You have been given grace and God's Word. Once you follow this pattern, your allegiance will be cemented in righteousness, and sin will no longer be able to control you.

AN APPETITE OF PLEASURE

"Sinful and forbidden pleasures are like poisoned bread; they may satisfy an appetite for the moment, but there is death in them at the end."

– TRYON EDWARDS

Pain, disappointment, struggle, and trauma all leave us gasping for the reward of pleasure. Innately, we make every effort to move out of the darkened state of mind into an emotional euphoria that wraps us in a bubble of dopamine that may only last for a moment.

I sought out pleasure hoping to escape my past, and my appetite for pleasure showed up in my promiscuous behavior. I always found myself right in a place I didn't want to be. It's hard to keep clean when you play in the dirt. It began to get old, and I felt there had to be more to life than this. It was hard to change my habits, but, as Jim Rohn said, "Reasons come first; answers come second." Curbing my appetite started when I set my mind on my future. I wanted a better life for myself and for my children, even though I didn't have any at the time. With the help of great friends, I was able to stay more focused each day.

In the summer of 2004, I started working with my best friend, Larry, in his company called Incisions. It was a health management company that was ahead of its time. This is where my love for teaching was birthed. As we studied health and consulted others on how to reduce sickness and disease in their lives, he began to see the correlation between the flesh, the spirit, and our appetites.

I once heard him say, "If a man can't say no to a honey bun; he might say yes to any kind of buns." That statement always stayed with me because, for as long as I can remember, I've had a sweet tooth. He was saying we are controlled in many areas of our lives by our appetites. If I couldn't say no to sweets or certain foods, which couldn't talk to me, how would I ever be able to resist the flesh of a woman I wanted?

I wish I had all the knowledge I gained that year back when I was in college. Shortly after he made that statement, I happened to watch a video about a lady who had cancer. She talked about how she had changed her diet and now her cancer was gone. I made a radical shift that day and decided to become a vegetarian. This one decision has helped me make the connection between what I put into my body and my spiritual growth. How I treat God's temple is in direct connection to how I treat my spirit. Now, I'm not saying you must be a vegetarian to begin to control your appetite, but you do have to be able to handle the small things to gain access to those things that are greater.

You say, "I am allowed to do anything"—but not everything is good for you. You say, "I am allowed to do anything"—but not everything is beneficial.

(1 COR. 10:23)

KING MAKER

I learned that my physical appetite is connected to my spiritual appetite. The discipline it took to let go of certain foods has helped me discipline myself spiritually in the areas of self-doubt, fear, failure, and sex. Just because you can do something doesn't mean you should. In 2004, I stopped eating all meat; I've never been back. Don't let your appetite for anything control you.

"In order for God to cover you, men, you are going to have to humble yourself under His authority. You are going to have to align your thoughts, actions, decisions, and leadership under the overarching viewpoint and authority of God."

—TONY EVANS

Years ago, they used to have a cartoon where an angel would appear on one shoulder and a devil on the other. Each would make an argument on why the character should do what he suggested. Eventually, it was up to the character to make the final decision. Sometimes, for me, it felt like there was a devil on either side. Whether you are young or old, there will always be an inner war led by the flesh, so, as men, we must learn to allow God to lead us in the Spirit.

At the end of Romans 7:25, Paul gives thanks to God for delivering him from the war that wages in his spirit. Growth and control will only come when we submit to God's way of doing things in our lives. Real men must learn to give the keys over to the best-designated driver the world has ever seen. Once I began to feed this portion of my spirit, I was able to conquer this area of my life. It took me a long time, but God is patient and he is faithful. Don't neglect your responsibility as king; Trust the King Maker.

W.O.W. #12 BE RESPONSIBLE

If you are going to be a king, you must be responsible. Many men walk away from their responsibilities as fathers because they have not been trained in the importance of being responsible. You must take responsibility for who you are and what you do. Knowing who you are in this world will guide you through this life—not as a helpless pawn but as a king who is a crucial piece in the entire game of life. Be responsible in whatever position you find yourself. Every male on the planet must graft inside himself the DNA of responsibility. Use your life to give God glory.

- **Be consistent** – The more consistent you are, the more others will be able to trust you. You build trust by being dependable.

- **Don't make excuses** – Prepare, plan, and practice. This will help prevent excuses. Work on yourself and don't make excuses.

- **Admit when you're wrong** – I learned how to confess two things that helped me become more responsible: "I was wrong" and "I don't know." I had learned to take ownership of my actions.

- **Don't complain** – Complaining only highlights the problem but working hard solves the problem. Think of ways to be grateful and help others.

- **Handle the small stuff** – If you ever what to get better and gain more responsibility, you must be able to handle the small things that have been entrusted to you. People won't give you more until they see that you can handle the small things.

CHAPTER 13

THE BLUEPRINT OF FATHERHOOD

———

When I became a father, I felt inadequate and unprepared to lead my family. Not that I was incapable of taking on the journey, I simply had no reference point or usable experience to model. I knew like Solomon I had to ask God for his wisdom and provision. Through my lack of fathering, I discovered God's true blueprint for the role a father must play in the life of his family and children.

BE PRESENT

"Tomorrow is jealous of today, so be present"

– K.JOYNER

The most important quality a father needs in order to have a lasting impact on his family and children is to be present. More than material things, a father's presence guides the trajectory of those they are connected to. Your presence is the dominant force that will help shape your child's understanding of the world they live in. It is crucial that you be there physically and emotionally. In a world where men are raised to be "tough" and not to cry, being open, vulnerable and transparent will help you develop a deeper relationship with your children. Your presence sends a message to your child's heart that you truly love them. Being there for them as they navigate this world empowers them to live life freely and unafraid. At times you will act as an encourager, but encouragement is temporary empowerment is permanent. Your presence stains the soul of your children and gives life to everything they do.

Being there means more than just your physical presence. I use to work two jobs. I would teach 6:30-4:00 pm, then work at UPS as a supervision from 6-midnight. I did this for about 4 years. Needless to say, when I was present, I wasn't really there. My body was there but my mind was always in the express checkout lane, only I had too many items in my head. Sleep was also my enemy. I never got enough, which meant I was never operating at my best in order to be the best I could be for myself, my wife, and my daughter. This also meant that I couldn't give my best at work. It was a never ending cycle until one day a shot of truth from my daughter woke me up.

It was her freshman year of college and she was all set to move in on a Friday. However, for whatever reason UPS wouldn't let me off. I explained to my daughter that her mom and her parents would help her move in on Friday, and I would be up on Saturday to move the remaining things in her dorm room. She agreed. In her sophomore year, I had to do something for the young men I was mentoring at the time, and I took off work. I didn't even think about how she might have felt. At the end of her sophomore year, I had the presence of mind to simply ask her, "how had I done that year as her father? Was there anything I could have done better?"

Be careful what you ask for.

With her head bowed and tears in her eyes she said, "Daddy, you promised me you would be there for me, and when you took off for the boys and you didn't take off for me, I felt like you chose them over me." My heart sunk deep within my body and at that moment I felt like a failure as a father. Here's where I grew. I didn't get angry. I listened and made a decision that the relationship with my daughter was more important than my feelings. Shortly after that, I left UPS and used that moment to strengthen my relationship with my daughter. You will never get time back, so make sure you invest it in the right things.

Imagine before and after every trip in your car, you had to do some major work on it. Eventually, you will get tired of that car, but if you didn't do the work you wouldn't get to your destination. Being a great father takes real work which will only come if you put the time in. Time is the most valuable commodity that we all have been given in this life. How we use it will determine our success or failures as fathers. How we spend our time will ultimately determine our legacy as fathers and the destiny of our children. What I lacked from my own father was his presence. I longed to have him validate me and assure me of my value and self-worth.

I could go in for days about all the statistics of what the absence of fathers does in the home, in the community, and in the personal, emotional, and academic life of a child, but I know you already know that. I will say that when a father is not present we leave our children open to receive a direct hit from the evils of this world, which ultimately will kill their dreams, still their purpose, and destroy their destiny. Men, we must put away our phones, cut the TV off, unplug the video games and engage with presence for our children.

W.O.W.- BE PRESENT

It was God who gave the man his image of Fatherhood. You cannot truly know what fatherhood is unless you are connected to your father in heaven. The Bible says in Ephesians 6:4, "Fathers, do not provoke your children to anger by the way you treat them. Rather, bring them up with the discipline and instruction that comes from the Lord." Your absence will ultimately give way to anger, doubt, lack of self-worth, bitterness, and resentment for the children you bring into this world. You don't become a father when the child is born, you become a father when you accept your role as a man who is walking in the awareness of whom God designed you to be. Your presence represents an assurance for your children that can only be given by you. BE PRESENT

BROKEN MEN

Every major structure—from monuments to skyscrapers, schools to homes, and stadiums to malls—has an initial blueprint before construction even begins. A blueprint is a plan for how the structure will be designed. Following the plan will, ultimately, get you to the designed outcome. But what if you had no plan or design? What if you had no reference point for what you were constructing or how to do it? Many of our men and fathers were once broken themselves, and, as a result, they find themselves in no position to help their children or even to be better fathers themselves. I used to be angry with fathers who wouldn't step up for their children or their families. Now I understand why we have absent fathers. There is no playbook for being a man or a father. There's no script to read or class you can take, and as Bishop T. D. Jakes once said, "It's hard to be a man." Many women, including my cousin Dionne, believe that the man is the foundation of the family and that his role, if not taken seriously, can change the destiny of his family forever.

Over the past twenty years, the importance of the male has been constantly diminished in our society. His very presence has been devalued, and his insight is often viewed as an afterthought. His way is often viewed as being wrong. Now, while some men deserve the criticism, many do not. We never hear about the great fathers, stepfathers, and men who are and have been there for their children. We don't often discuss how great men are positively affecting their communities and schools. Men are questioning their place in society like never before. With his psyche damaged, his position questioned, and his role now being redefined by society, every man finds himself in a broken state of existence. He is increasingly unsure of how to conduct himself in a relationship, in marriage, and with his children. He needs a blueprint. The only way to build great men and fathers is to follow God's blueprint.

PROTECT AND PROVIDE

In the Bible, God often refers to himself as a lion, which is designed to hunt and protect. He uses this comparison to show us that not only is he strong, but that he bears one of the greatest characteristics all fathers need—he is a protector. As important as it is to show strength, it is equally important to be a protector. God has designed every man with the ability to live out this characteristic for his family. Fathers were made to be the protectors or coverings for their families' emotional, mental, and physical well-being. I believe most men want to be great providers for their families but have been misled about exactly what this means. Being a provider has often been associated with being the breadwinner or making financial decisions for the family. Yes, this is part of it, but it is only a small part of the full equation. Raising four children by herself, my mom had to take on the role of the financial provider *and* fill in the gaps for us mentally, physically, socially, and emotionally. Although women have been leading households for years, this is not the way God intended it to be. Fathers were designed to work with mothers to provide in all areas of family development, not just the finances.

LEAN TOWARDS GOD

Proverbs 22:6 Direct your children onto the right path, and when they are older, they will not leave it.

One of the things I admire about my friend Misi is that in every way he leans toward God. He is married and has four beautiful children. I love the way he parents and is often playful in public with his children. He too grew up without his father being truly active and present in his life. He also lacked a true model of what fatherhood looked like. When I asked him how he was able to make it, and become such a great father himself, he said, "In everything that I have been through, God's word has cancelled out all the bad I have experienced." It reminded me that in everything we do we must as men continue to lean towards God.

PAY ATTENTION - OPEN YOUR EYES

"When our attention is on the present, our life is constantly renewed."

– DEEPAK CHOPRA

I was 27 years old in 1996 when I first held my daughter. In corner of my mind, I heard the voice of my stepfather saying "You ain't never going to be nothing!" Growing up without my father left me without a portion of my life's blueprint. There I was with little guidance of what it meant to be a man and even less of what it meant to be a father. No role models in my family lineage except my grandparents who would divorce after 30 years of marriage.

At that moment a deep cradle of fear and doubt filled my chest and I remember looking up and saying to God, "Help me, I can't do this without you." My walk with God was in its beginning stages. I truly had no clue how to be a father. More importantly, I was still learning how to trust God in every situation. Every day since, I have been trying to conform myself to his will in order to be the best possible husband and father I can be.

I'd like to tell you it has been easy, but it hasn't. One of life's greatest gifts is an experience. The more time we spend growing and learning from what happens to us, the more we are able to see God's presence in everything. In other words, let life teach you. I will tell you that it has been worth it. Through fear and failure, I learned it wasn't my job to decide what my daughter would be or how my wife would love me. I discovered it was my job to point my life towards Christ so they would see him in me and eventually follow.

TOUGH LOVE

The Bible says to "Bring them up with discipline and instruction that comes not from your own knowledge, but from God and his wisdom."

In a father's absence, children lack the discipline and the instruction of God's word. One of the first verses I taught my daughter was Hebrews 12:11, "No discipline is enjoyable while it is happening—it's painful! But afterward, there will be a peaceful harvest of right living for those who are trained in this way." Just before I received my mothers' discipline across my backside, she would often say, "This is going to hurt me more than it does you." I learned as I became a father that she was right. It often hurts us to discipline our children, but in the tough times of life, that discipline will reap a harvest of good decisions for them. God sets boundaries to help us grow, but without some form of discipline, we will always test the waters of disobedience. Growing up I had no boundaries and there were few things I wouldn't do or try. Many of these things often got me into trouble. I didn't want that for my daughter.

Be Responsible* - The bible says in Psalm 127:3-5, "Children are a blessing from God."

"No love is greater than that of a father for His son."

– UNKNOWN

One day, while riding with a friend to drop his son off to his son's mother's house I learned the true meaning and importance of having a father. As we drove to our destination I listened to my friend give his son a set of instructions on what to do when he arrived at his mom's house. I admired him because even though he wasn't with the mother of his child, he still was present for his son. He had given him some new clothes and of course, his son was excited. When we arrived once again he restated his instructions. His son nodded and we walked to the door. Here's where everything changed: When his mom opened up the door my friend's son looked back at him and said: "Bye, Daddy."

Just as he walked to the door another man stepped out and stopped him. He gave my friend's son a whole new set of instructions. Like the air was let out of a balloon, his son with his shoulders depleted dropped his head and walked slowly into the house. What moved me most was the look on his father's face when all of this was happening. He looked as though he too was completely deflated and I knew then I would never want anyone to have that kind of influence over my daughter. It is a father's responsibility to lead, guide and direct his children. Not saying mothers' can't do it, but they were never meant to do it by themselves. Fathers, no matter what, never abandon the responsibility of caring for your children.

W.O.W. #13 FINISH WHAT YOU START

Imagine now any structure without a strong foundation. The building is unbalanced. Its roof is caving in because of its instability. It has cracks along the edges and feels unsafe to inhabit. This would not be a place to send our children, yet if we are not present they will be forced to live life in these types of environments. As we examine a society where some men have not been protectors, providers, present physically or emotionally, or responsible we see a society that is crumbling in disaster in every area. Now is the time to scrap the plans that we have and begin to build a true and sustainable foundation with God's blueprint. We all must finish what we start.

CHAPTER 14

QUEENS

"Everyone has inside of her a piece of good news. The good news is that you don't know how great you can be, how much you can love, what you can accomplish, and what your potential is."

– ANNE FRANK

The full potential of our young girls who grow up without their fathers is often never realized. Fathers who are absent in the lives of their daughters often expose them to the full impact of life's most destructive paths. This often leads our queens to believe the lies that are spoken into their spirits by men who themselves were neglected by their fathers. They long for the acceptance and love from a father figure in hopes of experiencing what they missed out on as a child.

Some of the effects of this may manifest in the form of low self-esteem or self-worth. Even more severe damage may result in eating disorders. As they long for the love of their fathers, food becomes the vice they turn to for love. Obsessing over being the perfect size and looking like the stereotypical model, they use food as a substitute for the relationships they long for. Many don't understand, and it's not their fault.

Depression is also more likely to visit our queens as a result of absent fathers. Fear of abandonment and rejection often leads them to shut down emotionally. It's a never-ending cycle that can only be broken when men, fathers, and husbands begin to take their positions more seriously and intentionally make it a priority to be present with our queens. When fathers are absent for whatever reason, they take a piece of their daughter's heart and soul with them. As a result, they leave our queens on an everlasting journey in search of that which only the father can give—love and a true model of what a godly man should be.

When my daughter was born, I knew that, like King Solomon, I didn't possess the knowledge or wisdom to lead her properly. As a result, I called on God. My faith in him and his unwavering love for me helped develop me as a man, husband, and, most importantly, as a father. Ever since my daughter could talk, I warned her about the boys she would meet. I specifically told her never let a boy put his hands on you, never let them call you out of your name, and, most importantly, never let them define you. It may have been a little much for a six-year-old, but I needed her to be aware.

FAILING FATHER

When my daughter was in elementary school, she was severely bullied. Day after day, she was tormented by one young man in her class. Other kids would join in and still others would be the bystanders. He teased her about how she looked, her hair, and even how she talked. At times, he convinced her she wasn't beautiful or intelligent. She doubted herself and began to internalize pain, which affected her overall confidence and self-esteem. This went on for years, but I didn't really understand the impact it would have on her until later in life. What he did would haunt her well into her late teens.

Failure #1

There was a time in my daughter's life when I felt like I failed her as a father. I was so focused on work and making sure I became a great provider that I neglected to be her protector. All I knew was she was enjoying school and doing well. By the time I truly understood what was going on, the damage had been done. I must admit that, as a father, I wanted to destroy him and make him suffer ten times as much as he had made my daughter suffer. My wife would later tell me she feared I would have done serious harm to him. You see, the person I was then is not the person I am now. I still had that hate and killer instinct in me for anyone who dared to hurt my family. I was always determined that my daughter would never know the fear or anxiety I had felt when I was younger. Unfortunately, in this season of her life, I had failed her because I wasn't there for her.

Failure #2

Fast forward and now my daughter was eighteen. We'd gone through a difficult time when she was in middle school. As a father, I saw firsthand how our children can change right before our eyes. It was as if she was someone else's child. It was the season just before the prom, and, like any father, I knew this was going to be a big deal.

As fathers, whenever we meet the guy who wants to date our queens, we often think about what we had in mind when we were their age. I didn't like her date. As I sat him down to talk with him and put the fear of God in him, I knew in a matter of minutes that he wasn't the one for my daughter. As my wife, my daughter, and I were gathered at the table, I told him that he wasn't the one for her. Here's where it got tricky. Sometimes our queens can't see what we see as fathers. They think we are trying to steal all their fun. In reality, we are trying to save them much heartache and pain.

As their relationship progressed, it soured. It turned into an attack on her self-esteem and ended with plenty of tears and heartbreak. Now, while I wanted to do something I might have regretted, I will never forget when my daughter came to me and said, "Dad, it's over." As we sat on the couch, she cried with a deep burst of emotion I will never forget. In that moment, I thought to myself, *What if I wasn't here to catch her? What if I wasn't here to help her eventually regain the picture of who she truly was as a young lady?* I knew I should have stopped it a long time ago, but sometimes we've got to let God's plan play out so our queens know they can both trust us and count on us as fathers.

Over the years, our relationship has grown to a level that I thought was lost forever. She has made me more vulnerable and sensitive to both her feelings and my own. I'd like to think that through it all, she is as proud of me as I am of her. She took all the pain and began to push herself toward greatness. She never settles for anything less than what she wants in this life. She has developed into a queen of grace and elegance who I truly admire. Every day, I remind her that pain isn't wasted misery—it's a divine preservation of a future blessing. Through the grace of God, she now knows her name: **Queen**.

The relationship between me and my daughter is ever-evolving. We are closer now than we have ever been. I have learned so much from watching her meet and defeat the challenges of her life, and it has inspired me to a better man. We've had the tough conversations about me working too much and neglecting time with her. We've had conversations about life and boys. Most of all, we've had special talks about how proud I am to be her father and to see her live her life's purpose.

W.O.W. #14 FAILURE PRODUCES SUCCESS

If I hadn't failed during this time in our relationship, I wouldn't have been able to grow as a father. Men, don't beat yourselves up when you fail in this area. Learn from it, grow from it, and make a definitive plan to ensure that it never happens again. Your failure has the potential to produce your greatest success.

WEAR YOUR CROWN

"Think like a queen. A queen is not afraid to fail. Failure is another stepping-stone to greatness."

– OPRAH WINFREY

In 2007, when my sister Patrice told me I should write this book, little did we both know that it would take twelve years to manifest. Fast forward to 2019, and she has six beautiful children, her own dance company, and is truly making a difference in the lives of so many people.

Like me, her faith has shaped and matured her into a bold, dynamic woman of purpose. She has led her life with intention over the past twenty years. Her strength, like our mother's, is unprecedented. She lives the abundant life in Christ, not just attending church but living out the gospel daily.

Faced with so many disappointments and challenges over the past ten years, she has sacrificed her life for her children and given everything she can to help others. Her faith has been inspiring both to me and to others around her. She is truly a queen who lives life out loud and in color. Over the years, trials have changed her and pulled out her greatest accomplishments. Growing up without ever knowing her father, as with most young girls, has profoundly affected her. I know this is why family is so important to her. She wears a crown of faith.

To my queens, you are not a pawn in God's eternal plan. You are the missing piece to his master plan. No king can stand in his position without you. For how can a king claim a throne devoid of his queen? Your intuition is second to none. You are beautiful beyond your years, and you hold grace and elegance like pillars that support the legacy of families. Words cannot define you, and God hears your prayers daily.

Your lips drip with wisdom, and your heart has the power to heal this nation.

Remember, if you want to fly, you must let go of everything that holds you down. Your beauty is embedded from within and your strength is uncanny. I've learned from my mom that every woman must be strong enough to let go yet patient enough to wait for what she deserves. You are a gift from God, so you don't have to settle for anything less than his very best for your life. Every day, you light yourselves on fire so that the world can stay warm. No one can wear your crown except YOU!

Queens remember, chin up or the crown slips.

CHAPTER 15

PURPOSE

"The thief's purpose is to steal and kill and destroy. My purpose is to give them a rich and satisfying life."

(JN 10:10)

What is my purpose in life? This is perhaps one of life's most compelling questions. Why am I here? I had never seriously asked myself this question. For me, at this point, just being here was enough. I felt like because I had survived the attacks of all the fiery darts life had thrown at me, I was free to do what I wanted to do; this thinking was so far from the truth. Now, while I've quoted the first part of this verse several times before, I never thought that I could have a rich and satisfying life.

TRUST THE DESIGNER

Think about the first automobile or the first airplane. The designers had a specific plan for creating them, and this determined how they designed it. God, the greatest designer, also had a purpose for us and, thus, designed us specifically with the ability to fulfill our purpose. His word reminds us that we are fearfully and wonderfully made. Purpose is direct in its attainment and has a goal. Everything that has ever been created developed from the mind of its designer. Just as fish came with the ability to swim and birds came with the ability to fly, you and I came with the ability to carry out our purpose. You are not born to find your purpose; you were born with and for a purpose.

Jeremiah 29:11, my wife's favorite scripture, says, "For I know the plans I have for you... plans to prosper you and not to harm you, plans to give you hope and a future." God has no needs. He doesn't want for anything. His desire is that we know him, obey him, and trust him. He has the blueprint for all our lives. He's seen the beginning, the middle, and the culmination of his plans for our lives. These plans include our prosperity as we live our life's purpose and the hope of unseen faith to enjoy what he has predestined for us in the future.

When I was young, I really only wanted two things. First, I wanted all the money in the world. I thought because we grew up poor, having money would solve all our problems. Second,

I wanted to live forever. I guess we all want that in some way. We want our names never to be forgotten. Purpose, it is the Goliath of one of life's most revolving questions. Early on, I thought I knew my purpose — to be an NBA superstar. In fact, it wasn't until my early thirties that I truly considered asking God what he wanted me to do with my life.

Once I checked with the designer of my life, the broad picture I had painted began to have a more clear and defined view. I began to truly see and move in the direction of my purpose. Applying God's Word and embracing the full weight of what I believed he wanted me to do was the catalyst that transformed me. It was like I had been re-energized and everything in my life made sense. His Word provides power and direction for every area of our lives. God's portfolio is unmatched and limitless. His knowledge is and has been thousands of years ahead of everyone. His imagination created things we could never think of because he is the ultimate designer.

TRUE NORTH

Our first and most crucial purpose is to know and enjoy the fellowship of God. Before I could seek my own desires, I had to get to a place where my faith and trust in God came first. I had to make him a priority and trust in his divine plan for my life. Matthew 28:19-20 says, **"Go therefore and make** disciples of all nations, baptizing them in the name of the Father and of the Son and of the Holy Spirit, teaching them to observe all that I have commanded you. And behold, I am with you always, to the end of the age."

Purpose will hit you like a ton of bricks. I thought about all the years I had wasted trying to design my own life, when all I had to do was ask God. Over time, I realized I was made to give glory to my designer and that he was the true north I should always focus on for clarity and direction. These verses tell us that we are to be with him, obey him, and witness to others. It's not enough just to know God. As we journey through this life, enjoying God's love and grace, he also expects us to help others enjoy this same love by witnessing to them about our own life-changing experiences.

When I set my navigation system to reach a certain destination, it often tells me how far my destination is and how long it will take me to get there. It also lets me know about the road ahead and if there will be any delays along the way. What I love most is that if I am going in the wrong direction, it will immediately recalculate my arrival time and a new direction. Purpose gives you direction, and your direction determines your destination. God's purpose for our lives has a true north and will always place us on the right path. But unlike Waze, God's ways require faith. If you have ever felt you should be doing more with your life, now is the time to check your direction and ask yourself, "What is my purpose?" The only way to know is to look to the true north: God.

"Where there is hope in the future there is power in the present"

— ZIG ZIGLAR,

Hebrews 11:1, "Now faith is the substance of things hoped for, the evidence of things not seen."

Hope acts as a magnet as it pulls us through the tough times. The belief that we can and will prevail over our circumstances inevitably propels us to victory. Without hope, we die a slow death because life without hope is existence without meaning. True purpose can never begin as a result of our initial sight. We all hope for that which we don't see, and that is what makes life worth living.

Your purpose existed before you were born, but it cannot be fulfilled until you become selfless and live for something greater than you. The intentionality of God's craftsmanship is always directly linked to the assignment placed inside you. Living in an abusive home when I was young, I never gave up hope that one day we would have a better life. My purpose was buried under all the struggles I been through. The good news is your purpose is still within you. It may be buried underneath all the pain you have endured, but it's still there. Hope attaches itself to the future, and that is what God wants to give us.

GO ALL IN

When your purpose is unknown, you risk abusing your life. Knowing your purpose is important because when we don't know why we are here, we often engage in destructive activities that may temporarily derail our purpose. It's like going to the pool and only dipping your feet in along the edge; you can't say you've gone swimming. Until I went all in for God, I was indulging but was never a full participant. I had to cannonball into the deep in of the pool and immerse myself in the water to really say I had been swimming. That's what God wants from us. He wants us to go all in for him to discover why he made us and what we should be doing with our lives.

Finding my purpose taught me how to focus less on the complexities of life and more on the simplicities. Purpose makes it clear what you should say yes or no to. If your purpose is to be a doctor, you can clearly say no to being a firefighter. If your purpose is to go to college, you can clearly say no to selling or using drugs. Purpose, like wisdom, can only be given by God, for man cannot give wholeness to that which he did not create. Once you have been given your purpose, God will pour out in you a spirit that allows you to resist and conquer failure. The will to do comes from the knowledge that we can do all things through him who strengthens us.

Pursuing purpose will require being a living sacrifice for that which you have been assigned to do. When God told Moses to go and speak to Pharaoh, Moses gave God excuses. He was looking at what he couldn't do, but God was looking at what Moses could do. Moses was looking at his lack, but God was looking at his purpose. He made it simple for Moses when He said, "Tell them that I AM" sent you.

VISION

Your vision is one of the most dominant senses you possess, and, if lost, it heightens your other senses. As light passes through the cornea, it is refracted onto the lens of our eyes. Light then passes through the lens and is bent a second time, where it arrives at the retina and an image is formed. What's amazing is that because of the bending of the light, the image arrives at the retina upside down. Only when the information travels along the optic nerve is it reversed in the occipital lobe and seen clearly. Likewise, our life's purpose may be seen upside down when we view life through our own lenses. When I began to view things through the lens of God's Word, I was finally able to see my life's purpose manifest.

Who you are, how you see yourself, and your life's purpose are all connected to your vision. In 2010, while checking a text on my phone, something strange happened; I couldn't see it. It was blurred, and I thought to myself, *My font settings must be off.* I quickly called my daughter and asked her to increase the font on my phone.

As she looked at it, she began to laugh. "Daddy, it's already set to the highest font you have. Your vision is off. You need your eyes checked. You may need glasses."

No way, I thought. I was only forty. As I entered the doctor's office for the first time in forever, I discovered that she was right. As he placed my head on the mount and I looked through the phoropter, he began to move the lenses until my vision was clear. Now I could see without squinting or double vision. If you are confused about your purpose, check your vision.

THE UNOPENED GIFT

After knowing and fellowshipping with God, our second purpose is to use the gift he has placed inside each of us to achieve that which he gave us dominion over. Everyone is here for a reason, and we all have an assignment.

In your lifetime, how many gifts from birthdays, Christmas, Valentine's Day, and all the other holidays have you left unopened? How many gifts have you received without eventually realizing what they were? Almost all of us would say none. What sense does it make to receive a gift and not open it, or to open it and not know what it is? God has freely given you and me a gift, and we must use it to serve others and glorify him. (1 Pet 4:10-11) If you do not know what your gift is, you must consult the one who gave it to you. Once you know what your gift is, it must be cultivated and worked for it to grow inside of you.

When trying to put together an intricate puzzle with many pieces, it's best to always start with the outer edges and work inward. However, as we try to put together the pieces of our lives to develop a clear picture of our purpose, we must start from within. Inside all of us is a gift that will help us complete our assignment for God. That gift must be opened. Have you ever thought you were destined to do something else or that your life could have been so much more? Have you ever felt out of place, like you belong somewhere else? That feeling is called **the unopened gift!**

If you are in a place where your gifts and your purpose are not being cultivated to serve others and glorify God, you will always have that feeling. Most people aspire to live a comfortable life, never taking a risk for God but always taking a risk for everything else. If you have been praying for something and God has not delivered, it is because he sees that the one gift he left inside of you, the most important gift, remains unopened.

Most people focus on the gift and not the giver, and when you do this, you lose sight of the real blessings. Through trials, pain, disappointment, tragedy, anger, and frustration, God makes us appreciate the gifts in our lives. Here are some unopened gifts you can take advantage of now:

- Smile more, for it's the gate to your heart.
- Give more gifts.
- Be bold and trust God.
- Do the unexpected for someone.
- Never let the child in you die.
- Laugh at yourself.
- Pray for someone else's miracle.
- Listen and respect those who are older than you.
- Cherish the wonder growing in you as the only chance to assist God in a miracle.
- Talk less and listen more.
- Take more risks for God.
- Never react to abuse by passing it on.
- Never give up on your dreams—just get new ones.
- Say I love you and mean it.
- Never hold on to knowledge.
- Forgive one another.
- Choose your friends carefully.
- Seek to understand.
- Never say no to God.
- Dream big dreams and think greater thoughts.
- Take care of your body.
- Be humble.
- Speak the truth in love.

- Read more books.
- Let someone get in front of you in traffic.

Your unopened gift is your ticket to heaven, and that is the ultimate destination God has for us. God wants to see you return to him, but Satan does not. Satan only has the power we give him, and he knows if you open the gift inside of you, he will never be able to control your life. His only purpose is to get you to disqualify yourself from getting all that God has for you.

W.O.W. #15 DO YOU – DISCOVER YOUR PURPOSE

When you walk in purpose you become the very best version of yourself. You must become who you were designed to be. You are not a mistake. You are here for a specific purpose but satan wants to abort it. If you trust the designer, he will give you clarity and a vision for your destiny. God wants to give you a rich and satisfying life. Don't die with an unopened gift inside you.

CHAPTER 16

FIRST CLASS

———

*"Don't allow anybody to make you feel that you're nobody.
Always feel that you count. Always feel that you have worth,
and always feel that your life has ultimate significance"*

– DR. MARTIN LUTHER KING JR.

How do you see yourself? What is your self-image? Do you
see yourself through the thoughts and ideas of others? Are
you living in bondage by the judgment and insecurities
others have placed on you? The value we place on things
determines its level of importance in our lives. How we see
ourselves often determines the power and intention with
which we live our lives. Self-worth can never be bestowed
on us by people or material things; it must come from a deep
sense of knowing our own value that was given to us by God.

When we look at straw in a glass of water, it appears to be bent. What is really happening is that the light from the part underwater is refracted and seems to change direction. What we believe regarding our ability is often refracted but is not a true picture of who or what we can accomplish.

It seemed I'd been fighting the fear that I wasn't good enough ever since my stepfather told me I wouldn't amount to anything. What I learned to do is to use this fear to my advantage. It made me work even harder to ensure failure would never define me. The fear of not being my best drove me to imagine only the success of winning.

FAITH OVER FEAR

There are many ways to combat fear. **First, identify what you truly fear.** Is it embarrassment? Is it failure? Is it not feeling good enough or even a feeling that others won't or don't like you? Much of what we fear has to do with the unknown. We fear what we don't know or understand. The Bible says, *"To get wisdom, but though it cost you all you have, get understanding." (Prov 4:7).*

I began to study whatever I was afraid of. I made sure I understood what I was afraid and why. Through understanding, we take back the power that fear tries to snatch from us. Jesus had no fear of death because he knew it would not be his end, but his beginning. When you begin to understand your fear, you transition from being enabled to empowered.

Second, move in a different direction. They say insanity is doing the same thing and expecting a different result. You probably finished that sentence in your mind before actually reading it. This is because your brain automatically went in the direction that you most remember. To conquer fear, we must take what we perceive to be real and move in a direction contrary to that fear. Ever since I got married, I've been willing to try to move in a different direction to gain the positive results I desire. Moving away from the old toward the new will bring new insight and new opportunities for growth. Remember, those who are first class always reach for the best.

Finally, work hard on your vision. Your vision can produce what you want. It can give you dominion over fear. You must work hard to ensure that everything you do lines up with your desired outcome. Just as I used to visualize hitting the game-winning shot when I was seven years old, when the time came for me to make that my reality, I was able to do it. The vision I had worked hard on would eventually manifest itself in my life. If God did it for me, I know he can do it for you.

I used to have a terrible fear of flying. After taking my first flight in 1995 to Disney World to impress my girlfriend and now wife, I didn't fly again until I was headed to Chicago to appear on the Steve Harvey Show in 2016. Twenty-one years had passed, and now I had to face that fear all over again.

Today, because of my job, I'm on roughly thirty to forty planes a year. One day, while heading home to Charleston, South Carolina, from a connecting flight, I sat in the row just behind first class. It was the first time I had ever been that close, and I remember thinking, *When will I get the chance to sit in first class? Or maybe I'm just not first-class material.* That thought spoke to my state of mind.

I watched as the attendant walked the aisles to check on everyone, both in first class and in regular seating. We all received the same standard introduction and safety instructions. Shortly after takeoff, the attendant pulled the mesh curtain to close off the first-class section. I was amazed because I could see directly through the curtain, and it didn't seem like they received anything more than I did. I don't drink alcohol, so that didn't appeal to me. I got some of the same snacks and had plenty of legroom. Still, I thought to myself, "God, when will I get to fly in first class?"

Here's where I got what Squire Rushnell calls a *God Wink* moment. A God-wink moment, as he describes it, is what some people would call a *coincidence*. My great-grandmother used to say, "Coincidence is God's way of remaining anonymous." It can also be the answer to a prayer in a way that can come only from God.

On my connecting flight, just before boarding, the receptionist said, "Excuse me, sir. We have to change your seat."

I thought, *Why me and not someone else?*

She went on to say, "We have a family who wants to sit together, so we had to adjust your seat."

Now, to be honest, I wasn't feeling it, but then I thought to myself, *I'm headed home.* As long as I was on the flight, I didn't care.

Then she handed me the ticket, Priority First, Group 1, Seat 1F. In that moment, God winked at me and said, "You are already first class because I made you, and all you have to do is ask and I will take care of you."

As I took a selfie and sent it to my mom. All I could do was laugh.

What we believe shapes the thinking and vision for our lives. You must know who you are and that your identity is not, nor will it ever be, wrapped up in your appearance, intellect, status, or wealth. Your identity will always rest in the one who made you.

Remember, we are made in the image of God, fearfully and wonderfully made, chosen before the beginning of time, and recipients of an inheritance that no one can take from us. These are all things that have been given to us even though we may not deserve them. Develop ways to use fear and anxiety for your benefit. No matter what you've done, or where you come from, God wants you and I to always remember that we will forever be FIRST CLASS.

- **Self Love** – Embrace and Love the uniqueness that you possess; there is no one on the planet like you

- **Self Awareness**- Live confidently that you are God's masterpiece and he is always with you

- **Self-Acceptance** – Don't measure yourself by peoples opinions, Use God as the standard because he has already accepted you and made your perfect in his sight

PART IV

REDEMPTION

All of us want redemption. We want to be restored, repaired, vindicated, and rewarded. In short, we want to regain the value of that which we have lost. We want everything we have endured and sacrificed for to be worth it. While I can't tell you that everything will work out the way you want it to, I can tell you that no one redeems like God. His redeeming power transcends time and gives life to every situation. It started when he redeemed us and took our place on the cross, becoming a living sacrifice for all sin.

One of the most powerful stories I have ever read in the Bible is that of the prodigal son. God uses it to teach us about what redemption really means. In the story, a father has two sons. The younger, with all his hopes and dreams, asked the father for his share of his inheritance. The father agrees. Shortly afterward, the young man heads out to what the Bible refers to as "a distant country or foreign land," where he squanders his fortune. He is then reduced to working for the people of that country in a pigpen.

Then the Bible says that "he came to his senses." Like many of us, he found himself in a place he knew he was never designed to be. As a result, he conjured up a plan to return to his father to ask to become one of his servants. At this point, I thought the father would respond as many of us would, negatively. The Bible says that while he was still a ways off, his father saw him coming. This made me realize that his father never stopped looking for him. Filled with compassion and love, the writer says he ran to his son, embraced him, and kissed him. As the son humbles himself, he declares that he is unworthy to be his son. However, in pure joy, his father summons the servants to bring out the finest robe, ring, and sandals so his son would know of the joy his father feels for his return. His father throws a feast in celebration of the son and proclaims that his son who was dead is now alive; he was lost and now he has been found.

Jesus was trying to show us how we should react when even one of us returns to the Father. Redemption didn't occur when the son was in the pigpen, or even on the road home. I can imagine that he must have had his apology all planned out, but in the end, he didn't need it. Redemption occurred in the arms of his father. It was there that he realized the depth of the love his father had for him. In that moment, he understood what grace really was. True redemption and repentance can only occur in the embrace of God our father.

Therefore, say to the people of Israel: "I am the Lord. I will free you from your oppression and will rescue you from your slavery in Egypt. I will redeem you with a powerful arm and great acts of judgment. I will claim you as my own people, and I will be your God. Then you will know that I am the Lord your God who has freed you from your oppression in Egypt.

(EX 6:6-7)

Here are some benefits of redemption:

- God wants to bring us out of whatever has us in bondage or separates us from his love. He wants to sanctify us through grace and mercy no matter what we have done.

- He wants to free us from slavery. Not only does he want to bring us out of Egypt, but he also wants to take Egypt out of us. Sometimes we have desires and thoughts that keep us in bondage even though the cage is wide open.

- God wants to redeem us in such a way that we receive all the promises he has for us. Our purpose and abundant life have already been predestined for us, and God wants to restore us to his original plan for our lives. However, because God is such a gentleman, he will never force himself into our lives. He can and will deliver us out of any situation.

- God wants to make us his people. He desires a relationship with us beyond anything. I never knew if God would redeem my life and give me what I longed for, which was a real relationship with my father. I could only hope to one day to experience his redemptive love, which is the only thing that can restore, revive, and replenish our souls.

CHAPTER 17

YOU ARE A MIRACLE

"Miracles are a retelling in small letters of the very same story which is written across the whole world in letters too large for some of us to see."

— C.S. LEWIS

It's a miracle I made it out of all the things that could have destroyed my life. To beat the odds of all the statistics that were laid before me is a miracle. The good news is that what is possible for one is also possible for another.

When people say, "it's a miracle" what they are really saying is that they can't conceive with their natural minds what has taken place in the physical realm. A miracle in its basic form is said to be a divine event that transcends human ability or thought and cannot be explained through natural interpretation. When we experience something that we have never seen before on this planet we deem it; a miracle. ***Here's the reality, you are a miracle.***

Your very existence is in fact, a miracle. The chances of you being born are one in 400 trillion. You have a better chance of being struck by lighting three times in a year opposed to being born. You are not a mistake. It is important that you understand your miracle status in order for you to realize the redemptive power your life represents.

The model we see of our father's can change our lives forever. Growing up without her biological father, my co-worker's story truly is a miracle. All of her life she had never met her biological father and for a long time thought that he had passed away. Unlike many, she never felt as though she had missed out on anything because of the great role model she had in her stepfather. She credits him for setting the standard of excellence and love that she now carries throughout her life. It was his selflessness and commitment to her and her mother as well as his commitment to God that gave her a solid foundation of faith that would eventually lead her to develop a relationship with her biological father.

This incredible journey started with a simple desire to trace her original heritage. A small gift from her husband in the form of an Ancestry DNA Kit led her to discover that her biological father was still alive. After believing for more than 15 years her father had passed away, the DNA kit revealed that she was a close match for two other people that she would soon meet. After making a new connection with two people who would turn out to be her cousins, more curiosity set in for everyone. Deeper inquiry revealed that there was a DNA connection between her and an unknown person who turned out to be her father. This new family along with a father she had never know welcomed her in with open arms. The celebration grew a bond that will forever be indestructible. Discovering that she comes from the lineage of truly amazing people has crystallized her faith and affirmed what God had already predestined. We are all miracles.

YOU HAVE WHAT YOU NEED

Peter 1:3 -By his divine power, God has given us everything we need for living a godly life. We have received all of this by coming to know him, the one who called us to himself by means of his marvelous glory and excellence. 4 And because of his glory and excellence, he has given us great and precious promises. These are the promises that enable you to share his divine nature and escape the world's corruption caused by human desires.

After you come to the realization that you are a miracle, you can rest in the assurance that everything you need to live a successful life, you have already received from God. It wasn't until I truly understood that I wasn't given some of the things I needed to live a great life, but God had already given me *everything* I needed that I truly began to see, as I said earlier, that life was not happening to me, but for me. Everything we face in life that tries to destroy or derail our hopes and dreams will never be as powerful as what God has already placed in us. Remember, we don't have to live as victims because of what we've gone through in life. God has already given us the victory if we use the power he gave us.

HAVE FAITH

Hebrews 11:1 Now faith is the substance of things hoped for, the evidence of things not seen.

Perhaps the single most important weapon that we've been given to overcome everything we face in this world is our *faith.* Early on in life, faith was something that I had heard people talk about but I never truly understood what it was or even how to use it. It seemed like this elusive supernatural power that only a few could tap into.

Looking back, it was just the opposite. Faith is a free gift from God given to all of us in order to help us live a life filled with purpose. One of the key ingredients in faith is *hope*. Hope breathes life into every situation. It sees possibility when confronted with impossible odds. It infuses life into dead thinking. Hope finds a way out of no way. It helps single mothers work two jobs and go to school in order to produce a better life. It gives power to women who have suffered from infertility and miscarriages only to see a child born to them later in life. Hope takes kids who were born in to poverty and makes them billionaires. Hope as the bible says does not disappoint us. It is the catalyst that sets our faith in motion.

But what happens when we lose hope? How then do we believe in what we cannot see? I often felt trapped inside a bubble filled with my goals, dreams, and ambitions for the future, yet devoid of hope I allowed fear, doubt, shame, and my current surroundings to squeeze the life out of my faith. Sometimes, one of the most difficult things to do in life is to believe and trust God for things that we have never seen, or seen others accomplish. I believe this is why God's greatest blessings require crazy faith.

FAITH - USE ONLY AS DIRECTED

"Use as directed" appears on just about every prescription bottle given to any patient today. When you don't use the medication the way it was intended to be used, you risk a chance of unfavorable outcomes. The same is true with our faith. If we don't use it correctly, we risk the chance of not experiencing God's promises. Faith, at its core is the tangible reality of things we cannot see.

"Faith is acting like God is telling the truth"

- TONY EVANS

In 2010, I tore my Achilles playing basketball. It was one day before I was set to do my final semester of student teaching. I couldn't believe it. My last semester and now I was out for at least 7 months. As the months went on, I started an intense rehab in hopes of returning before the entire year was lost. I couldn't work, or drive and so, for the first time in over 30 years, I couldn't do for myself. I had to depend on others.

One day, about 3 months into my rehab, I asked the therapist how long I had before I could go back to work and school? She looked at me and said, "Until you can put your full weight on it, I can't release you. Therapy often made me feel like a kid who was learning how to walk all over again. I didn't trust myself and I certainly couldn't put my full weight on it for fear of collapsing. This is how faith works. What we say we desire must be coupled with a belief that is so strong that we are willing to put our full weight on it, even when we can't see how things will work out. If you believe in something, exercise your faith by going all in and moving with an assurance in the direction of your desires. In every situation we face, trusting God get's easier every day because he always comes through for us. When we put our full weight on what God wants for our lives; he will release it. Real faith always gets God's attention.

Hebrews 11:6 And it is impossible to please God without faith. Anyone who wants to come to him must believe that God exists and that he rewards those who sincerely seek him.

W.O.W. #17 WALK BY FAITH

Walking by faith will require the ultimate trust in God's word. Like Noah, you may often have to walk alone. It may cost you some friends and you may feel abandon at times. At some point you will have to give up control of your life and trust in that which you can not see. This walk will pull you out of your comfort zone and place on a tight rope with no net below you. It will require constant sacrifice and obedience, but the reward will be like nothing you have ever seen before.

- **You have been given power** - God's power has the capability to solve every problem we face; faith helps you stay connected to him, in order to receive his power.

- **You have been given a promise**- Jeremiah 29:11 *For I know the plans I have for you," says the Lord. "They are plans for good and not for disaster, to give you a future and a hope.* God knows your beginning, middle and end. He has a plan to prosper you and he wants to give you a hope and a future.

CHAPTER 18

SECOND CHANCES

"When it comes to God, we can't run out of second chances only time."

– ROBIN JONES GUNN

LEARN AND GROW

You may have heard people say, "If I knew then what I know now, I would have made a different decision." Living with regret is one of the painful aspects of life simply because we can never fix it. However, occasionally, the coin of life flips over for us.

In 2018, something that never happened before took place in the NCAA tournament. My old school, UMBC, shocked the basketball world as the first sixteen-seed to beat the then-number-one seeded Virginia Cavaliers. It was complete euphoria for the retrievers of UMBC and complete devastation for Virginia. Not only would they be known as the first number-one seed to fall in the first round of the tournament to a number sixteen seed, but they would have to go the rest of their lives with the regret of losing on the biggest stage of their lives.

What stayed with me was the grace and class displayed by the head coach, Tony Bennett, and his players. When discussing the loss, they didn't point fingers or shift blame. They took responsibility for what had happened, and, for a year, they faced the questions of that loss. How sweet it was when, just a year later, having dealt with all the questions, comments, tweets, newspaper articles, and negative fanfare, this same team and coach won the National Championship. Virginia took full advantage of their second-chance opportunity.

This is an example of what God wants to do for us all. Redemption destroys regret and allows us to take devastating disappointment and turn it into a force which propels us to victory. As part of my purpose development, God had me mentoring youth in my church in the late '90s. One day at Payne Memorial AME Church, I conducted a mentoring session for our group, called Boys to Men. I told them how important education was for the future they wanted.

Knowledge would be the power that propelled them out of their current environments and into a life filled with options, and I let them know I wanted every one of these young men to go to college. Now that I was an adult, married with my own child, I knew far too well that what everyone had been telling me when I was growing up was true.

In the middle of my talk, a young man raised his hand. I continued to push into my main point about college, but he seemed to be losing his patience. Since his hand was still eagerly raised and he was halfway out of his seat, I reluctantly stopped and called on him. His question would change my life forever.

He said, with a slight attitude; "Did you finish college?"

Like a piercing blow to my heart, that one question illuminated one of my greatest regrets. It stopped me in my tracks. You see, life had hit me, and when my daughter was born in 1996, the choice came down to school or work to feed my family; I chose my family.

After what seemed like forever to me, amid the silence, with my head down and feeling defeated, I said, "No, I didn't." Like a fighter who had just thrown the punch that would cause his opponent to fall, he threw his second punch, which felt like a body blow from Mike Tyson.

"How are you telling us about going to college and you didn't even finish?"

That was the knockout blow to my soul. All I could say was, "Just stay in school."

That night, like a weight on my brain, that whole scene played repeatedly in my spirit. I felt frustrated and angry. In this season of my life, I had given up on the possibility of going back to school.

NEW LIFE

Thank God for second chances. In 2007, my wife asked me for the fifth time to consider moving to South Carolina. Her parents had retired and moved back to the south. Shortly afterward, as mentioned earlier, her mom was diagnosed with breast cancer. We made the trip from Maryland to South Carolina so many times in the dead of night. In my spirit, I never wanted to say no, but after a conversation with her mom, I made the decision to trust God and go all in.

I will never forget that as her mother was on the eve of enduring her first day of chemotherapy, she said to me as we stood in the kitchen, "The same God that takes care of you in Maryland, will be the same God that takes care of you in South Carolina." In a complete exodus from Maryland, we sold everything and began a journey that would change my life forever. During this time, I was a supervisor working for UPS. I had put in for a transfer, but the only way they would transfer me to another state is if I was enrolled in school. There I was at thirty-eight years old, almost eleven years after I had left, embarking on my second chance to fix one of my greatest regrets. I never thought it would happen, but it did.

The journey was tough; however, with this second opportunity, God gave me a different focus and a new resolve. Working 3 a.m. to 9 a.m. and taking nineteen credits my first year was unthinkable at times. I was the oldest person in all my classes every year for four years, but it didn't matter. I was on a mission to prove to God and everyone I could do it. What others thought was a lot of work, I saw through my second chance lens as a great opportunity. I welcomed the late nights and early mornings, knowing that, through it all, God was with me.

PLAY UNTIL YOU WIN

"I've grown most not from victories, but from setbacks. If winning is God's reward, then losing is how he teaches us"

— SERENA WILLIAMS

In 2012, I entered my final semester of college with just one final praxis test to take to complete my degree. I felt closer to my destiny than ever before. I remember talking with my advisor, Dr. Bone, and telling her I was ready to be a teacher and to have my own classroom. We were both excited, not knowing there would be one final roadblock. I had studied for this test, which was obviously the most difficult one yet. The praxis was a two-hour exam that you had to pay to take. It was the final piece of the puzzle I needed to complete the second chance God had given me.

I had already failed it twice, and the advisors had made it clear that we would not be able to walk if we didn't pass the test. Anxiety overwhelmed me, and I failed it again. I wasn't worried. I still had time to take it again before graduation in May 2011. Two weeks before graduation. I went to take the test again. The test was timed and had a running clock you could see with each question. I knew I needed a 164 to pass. After two hours, I clicked the last question and the test shut off. Just seconds after I finished, my score flashed on the screen—163.

I couldn't believe it. Like a kid whose emotions overtake him during a defeat, my eyes welled up and I wanted to cry right then. I jumped out of my seat in frustration, walked out of the room, signed the log, and walked out of the building. My wife and daughter had driven me to the test and were waiting in the car when I walked out. With my eyes full, I opened the door and dropped into the seat with all my disappointment and cried like a baby. I hadn't cried like that since the untimely death of my grandmother. It hurt so bad.

I would eventually fail the test six times and fall into a deep depression. During this time, the fear, doubt, and uncertainty would take me back to the voice in my head that had echoed for so long: "You ain't never going to be nothing!" Two days later, I got a call from my mom and didn't pick up. She left me a voicemail, which I still have to this day. It simply said, "Keep trying. Don't ever give up."

My great-grandmother would often say, "Baby, it came to pass; it didn't come to stay."

Failure often produces success. All adversity will eventually come to an end in time. What seems like forever may only be a season, and God will always provide strength to bear whatever we face. Even before we moved south, I had formed a bond with my wife's father. He had seen me through some tough financial times and had been there for me in my time of need. He had heard of my disappointment, and as we rode to the store one day, he handed me the money to take the test again. At first, my pride wouldn't let me take the money, but he said, "I believe in you, and I know you're going to pass that test." Without telling anyone, including my wife, I signed up to take the test again. You see, if I failed, no one would know but me. I didn't want to let him down, so I studied like never before.

I read the story of Job before I left to take the test and marked my Bible at 2:15 p.m. Feeling that same anxiety, I stepped into the testing center scared but prepared. As the test came to a close, I was so nervous my heart began to pump Kool-Aid. Then it happened: the score popped up, 173.

On September 15, 2011, my adversity ended. Six times I had walked out of the same testing center feeling worse each time, but on that day, with my heart full, I stood up, thanked God, and joyfully signed the log. The same lady who had seen me walk out several times before glanced at me and said, "You did it!" I walked out the testing center and jumped in my car and cried, but this time it was a cry of joy and laughter, with sloppy tears, excitement, and relief I had never felt before.

That day, when my wife and daughter got home, I sat them both down on the small brown couch and simply said, "I passed." They were in shock, and we all cried that sloppy cry again. We quickly jumped into the car and drove to my wife's parents' house to tell them the great news. Jubilation rang out from her mom, and even her dad, who is normally subdued and quiet, let out a laugh of thankfulness, with a hug that only a father could give a son.

Finally, the day came for graduation. With my mom, my brothers and sisters, best friends, and cousins in attendance, I was set to receive the final gift of the second chance I had been given. As I walked across that stage, I was finally able to kill the voice in my head that had held me captive for so many years—the voice of my stepfather that said I would never be anything. *That day, I buried it forever.*

W.O.W. #18 PLAY UNTIL YOU WIN

It's not over until God says so. Whatever you don't destroy will eventually come back to crucify you. You must grow to a place where your past doesn't come back to choke your future. God's wisdom and patience must not be taken for granted. Take advantage of your second chances. No matter what you have been through or what you have done; God can give you a second chance. I've learned that when you get a second chance, it's never about you. It will always be connected to your purpose and your destiny. Your story of victory will be the fuel for someone else's success. Don't ever think you're weak. Don't ever say you're weak. Most importantly, don't ever believe you're weak. If you rise for a new day, God is giving you a second chance. Please make sure you use it. Play this game called life until you win!

CHAPTER 19

BREAK THE CYCLE

———

Millions of children grow up without their fathers, a cycle I was determined to break when I became a father. The question is how do we break this cycle of fatherlessness that has plagued our society for so long? How do we build strong men and plant them back into their homes, schools, churches, and communities? Most of all, how do we place them back into the lives of the children who so desperately need them? I believe fatherlessness is the most harmful demographic trend of this generation. It is castrating families at an unprecedented rate. Many people would say shake it off, man up, let it go, and tell me to move on from my negative feelings about not having my father in my life. As I said earlier, it doesn't just go away. I didn't know how to live my life outside of myself. I just couldn't let it go.

Breaking the harmful cycles of any addiction requires a complete shift in thinking and total trust in God. If you could change on your own, you would have already done it. We all need a helper greater than ourselves to completely break the cycle. It's estimated that one in three children under the age of eighteen lives without their fathers in the home. In addition, 63 percent of all suicides come from fatherless homes, and 85 percent of youth in prison come from fatherless homes.

Every year, addiction to alcohol, tobacco, illicit drugs, and prescription opioids costs the US economy upwards of $740 billion in treatment costs, lost work, and the effects of crime. The statistics are overwhelming, and many of the problems we face as a society can be traced to the lack of fathers in the lives of their children. The effects have lasting consequences, and they found themselves on my doorstep when I least expected it.

LIFE CYCLE

Early one morning in the summer of 2001, I got one of those calls that leave a hole in your heart because you know something is wrong. I didn't answer on the first ring or even the second. Finally, with anxiety forming a path from my mind to my hand, I picked up the phone.

My uncle Earnest said with a deep breath, "Kenny, I need you to meet me at the hospital in Takoma Park, Maryland. It's your dad."

As I raced to the hospital from my apartment in Glen Burnie, I thought to myself, *What now?* You see, earlier that month, my dad had retired from his long-time government job at the Department of Treasury and had taken ill. As a result, I was asked to be his power of attorney. I didn't particularly want this role, but he needed me at the time.

One day, I went to pay his rent, and the clerk said to me, "Mr. Joyner, I don't know what's going on with your father, but for some reason, he is determined to drink himself to death!"

With a disappointed look on my face, I was at a loss for words and simply said, "Thank you." I walked out with my head down, not understanding things were about to get even worse.

Fast forward, as I arrived at the hospital, I was greeted by my uncle, who abruptly pulled me to the side and told me the severity of my dad's drinking problem.

"I'm not sure if you understand just how long your dad has been dealing with his drinking problem," he said.

He was right; I wasn't.

"I found him passed out in front of his apartment building," he said, shaking his head in disbelief.

As I walked into the room and saw my father lying there, I didn't know what to think. Little did I know it wouldn't be the last time I would see my dad in a hospital bed. I was concerned, but the emotional switch that turns on the lights of empathy and sympathy had been burnt out from years of bitterness and resentment. I didn't want to see anything happen to him, but I just didn't have sympathy in me at the time.

"Nothing records the effects of a sad life so graphically as the human body"

— NAGUIB MAHFOUZ

Shortly after I walked into the room, the doctor asked me to step outside. He said something I had never heard before. First, he asked me how old I was.

"Thirty-two," I said.

"Have you ever been tested for the alcoholic gene?" he asked.

At the time, I didn't even know there was such a thing. He then went on to say that one of my dad's kidneys was failing and that he was dealing with psoriasis of the liver as a result of his long-time addiction to alcohol. There I was thirty-two years old, facing a possible genetic connection to my father's long-time addiction. His life was still affecting mine, and there was nothing I could do to change it.

FREE TO CHOOSE

Freewill serves as a blessing and a curse for us all. God placed in all of us the power to choose because of his unselfish love for us. Just think, you and I have an unlimited number of choices we can make each day, and yet God only wanted us to make one choice: Him.

The cycle of any addiction is so powerful. It is not only a physical addiction but a physiological connection that over-powers the strongest of men and women. The cycle starts as a small yet corrosive vice, which will eventually dominate its host. Addictions cut through race, ethnicity, and gender. They range from drug use to shopping, from alcohol to eat-ing. No one is immune, and no one has the capacity to quit without help.

So how did I make it to thirty-two at that time without ever taking a drink? Some may call it luck, but now I call it grace. I saw early on what drinking could do to a man by watching my stepfather. I saw my grandfather also go several rounds with alcohol and lose. I lost a classmate in my senior year who was drinking and driving, and I had my own example in my dad as a strong testimony never to indulge in alcohol. This doesn't mean I didn't have a vice. I did. I was just determined not to let alcohol become an abuser in my life. My stepfather would drink, and now my father was suffering from the same addiction. I think I hated my stepfather as much as I grew to hate alcoholism. That hate made me never want to drink or even be around alcohol.

I never got the test done, I simply trusted God to help me continue to break the cycle. To this day, I don't carry not drinking alcohol as a badge of honor; I carry it as a burden of proof that God can break the cycle of any addiction.

SIN CYCLE

Sin also has a cycle. The Bible says in James 1:14-15, "Temptation comes from our own desires, which entice us and drag us away. These desires give birth to sinful actions. And when sin is allowed to grow, it gives birth to death."

I knew that if I was going to break the cycle of fatherlessness in my child's life, I had to trust a power greater than myself. You see, I had followed the cycle of sin on several occasions in my life. In fact, there have been times when I planned to sin on purpose. Knowing God and who he was, I still willingly went against his Word. I was addicted. I had to learn the stages of sin and addiction to reach a different outcome.

First, the initial and innocent association with sin. We are enticed and entangled through our own desires. In other words, we want what we want. Once we indulge sin, our spirits become tolerant to its overwhelming distortion of truth, and, subsequently, an addiction forms. Addictions with no restraint quickly turn into abuse, and abuse leads directly to dependence. This then crystallizes and the cycle begins to repeat itself unconsciously. Sprinkle in the effects of the brain, such as dopamine and the physiological connections, and you have an unbreakable bond that steals the soul of a person right up until their death. God has allowed me to become the type of father to my daughter, goddaughters, and godsons that I never had. God is no respecter of persons, and what he did for me, he can and will do for you.

Breaking the sin cycle will test your character, and your character is not like a coat you take off when things get warm in your life. Your character is like your skin, you can't take it off; its who you are.

BRING THEM BACK

There are two key areas in our society where children rarely see men active — in the home and in our schools. First, we need them in our homes. A devastating trend began some fifty years ago when we began to see more single-parent households rise throughout the country. As a result, more weight has been placed on our mothers financially, socially, and emotionally. Mothers and fathers are having to play the part of both roles needed for parenting, and our children are suffering. Asking them to bear this weight individually has changed our world forever. According to the US Census, there are more than 16.4 million children living in the US with a single mother, and 3.25 million living with a single father. This trend has continued to rise since 1970.

As I look back over my educational experience, I rarely remember having a male teacher. It wasn't until college that I began to see some diversity in this area. As a former educator, I remember being one of only three males during my teaching career. As I travel the world training teachers, I rarely see men in our schools. It has a profound effect on children when men are absent in these crucial areas. Education sets the foundation for academic success and dramatically affects behavior. We've got to bring them back if we are ever going to break the cycle of behavior issues we see in our schools. Fathers, we need you.

W.O.W: #19 LEAVE A LEGACY

Don't let your past define you, but let it mold you into the person you want to be. Our children will follow the example we set regarding how to live. Live life with passion and gratitude. Showing that we care for our children plants the fuel for life in them and, ultimately, helps them succeed. Give your family the gift of time. Being present changes the atmosphere in every home. Pass the baton of wisdom to your children. Their legacy will depend on what you give them in knowledge. Show your children what unconditional love looks like daily. Thank you to every father who has stood in the gap for his children and the children of others.

CHAPTER 20

THE WHOLE TRUTH

———

Jesus said to the people who believed in him, "You are truly my disciples if you remain faithful to my teachings. And you will know the truth, and the truth will set you free."

(JOHN 8:31-32)

When witnesses take the stand in court, they are asked, "Do you swear to tell the truth, the whole truth, and nothing but the truth, so help you God?" Attorneys then question them hoping to get the truth.

OBEDIENCE

My whole life, I had questions I wanted to ask my father, and, thankfully, I got the chance. Growing up without him left a hole in my heart. It also left me with more questions than answers. By the time I was in my late thirties, I had reconciled that my relationship with my dad had grown as far as it could. I had no desire to travel down that emotional roller coaster in hopes of gaining his love and acceptance. Buried inside my consciousness was the thought that I could move on permanently and close that chapter in my life. I was wrong. God often uses real-life experiences to expose the truth that lies deep within our hearts.

In late April 2015, I got a call from my cousin Eric, who had recently moved in with my dad, and I knew something was seriously wrong. One day he found my dad having what appeared to be an alcoholic seizure. He immediately called the ambulance, and they rushed my dad to the Washington Hospital Center. After hearing the news, I didn't know what to think. I was afraid I wouldn't make there in time to see him. I called each day for about a week to get an update, but each day, the news was worse.

My father had entered the hospital on April 28, and now, a week later, his condition wasn't improving. After talking with my sister Laval and learning more about his condition, I finally decided to make the drive from South Carolina to Washington DC. When I arrived, I couldn't believe what I saw. He was barely conscious, in a small, dimly lit room. His hands were bandaged, and he had a tube down his throat. His face was swollen to the point where he looked almost unrecognizable.

In that moment of uncertainty, all the missed birthdays and special occasions didn't matter. I didn't care that he had never seen me play ball in high school or even that he had missed my prom and my graduations from high school and college. All that mattered was that I didn't want him to die.

Over the next month and a half, I made the trip at least four times. On my third visit in late May, my aunt Teresa decided to come with me. They had moved him to another room in the hospital, and we entered his room, which looked like it hadn't been clean in days. It smelled of old urine and the trash was overflowing. My aunt demanded that they clean the room and change my dad's bandages and urine bag.

Shortly after they had completed all the cleaning, my dad's condition took a turn for the worst. The doctor said he had developed an infection and needed a blood transfusion. I didn't know what to do, but I knew I had to be obedient to God's Word, which says, "Honor your father and mother. Then you will live a long, full life in the land the Lord your God is giving you" (Ex 20:12). I had to make the call even though before all of this, I hadn't seen him in over three years. I gave the go-ahead, and within moments, the doctor and nurses all rushed in and rolled my dad into the emergency room.

While all of this was going on, my former pastor in Baltimore had asked me to preach the Father's Day service that year. I was honored and worried. Would I be preaching a sermon or perhaps planning a funeral for my dad? Over the next few weeks, God began to do something amazing inside of me. As I read Scripture to my dad, even though he couldn't respond to me, I could feel God filtering out all those years of anger, bitterness, and resentment. God was using this terrible time in my dad's life to wash away all the years of regret and replace them with a life-changing desire to renew our connection as father and son.

A piece of me called pride wanted to hang on to all those past feelings, because they gave me the platform to vent my anger. I never even thought about my dad's side. Over time, God began to restore my dad's health. After they adjusted the tube lodged in his throat, he began to eat more and started gaining his strength back. Next, through therapy, he was able to have his bandages removed from his hand and, eventually, he was able to feed himself. In the next few weeks leading up to the day I had to preach, he regained his speech and the overall movement of his feet and legs. Still, I had not seen him out of the hospital bed since late April.

NOTHING IS WASTED

As I arrived at the church on Father's Day to preach, I had my dad on my mind and God in my heart. I couldn't believe I was returning to Payne Memorial AME Church to stand in the pulpit after having left eight years ago to move to South Carolina. During the ten years we had attended this small church in Baltimore, I grew spiritually like never before as a husband, father, and a leader. The place was full and several of my friends and family were sitting in the front row.

I saw how God was using every experience I had gone through to help me that day. All that I had gone through manifested in the message. Ironically, I talked about fathers and how important it was for them to stand up for their children. Whenever I speak or preach, I feel physically drained afterward, but on this day, I felt fulfilled and restored. All that I had been through had prepared me for this day.

Once we left the church, we headed straight for the hospital. I couldn't wait to see my dad and tell him how things had gone. After all these years, I still wanted and needed my dad to be proud of me. Much to our surprise, he was not only awake but, for the first time since April 28, he was able to walk on his own. To say it was a miracle is an understatement. If I hadn't lived it for myself, I wouldn't believe it. I had seen him come all the way back from a place of hopelessness. God has used these moments to not only restore our relationship but to cultivate a new and deeper relationship with him. We never grow in good times, but when life challenges us, we grow exponentially. Nothing is ever wasted when God is trying to develop us.

And we know that God causes everything to work together for the good of those who love God and are called according to his purpose for them. *(Rom 8:28)*

FORGIVENESS -NOW I SEE

When Job was afflicted after enduring all he could from his wife and his friends, he questioned God. Job wanted what I wanted—answers. He wanted answers on why he had to deal with all the pain and suffering. I wanted what many young men want today, answers from their fathers on why they weren't there for them. Most people say we should never question God. As I read the story, I noticed God allowed Job to question him, but then God gave Job an answer that changed Job's understanding of who God was. Job responded by saying, "I have heard of you by the hearing of the ear, but now my eyes see you" (Job 42:5). Job understood God and saw him differently because of his suffering.

True forgiveness comes in not only letting go of the offense but forgetting it altogether. "I forgive you, but I will never forget" is what we often say to those people who hurt us. This really means, "I can't fully forgive you because I will never allow myself to forget." I needed God to help me forgive my dad and show me how to truly forgive. I could never have written this book if I had not reached this point in my life. When I forgave my dad, I not only freed him from his guilt and shame, but I also freed myself from the bondage of always feeling incomplete.

When I questioned my dad, he told me, with his heart filled with love, the whole truth of why he wasn't there. He talked about the shame and guilt that held him captive for so many years. He talked about his addiction. To my surprise, he talked about the joy he felt knowing he had a son. While fighting in the Vietnam War, the one thing that kept him alive was his hope of seeing me again. He never forgot me, and he never stopped loving me. *This was the truth I had never heard him speak before. At that moment, trying to hold back the tears, I felt like Job—now I see.* Just like the prodigal son, we embraced and our relationship had been redeemed.

Now I know that many have been unable to reconcile with their fathers for whatever reason. Some may never get the opportunity. However, if your biological father is still alive, you still have a chance to restore that which is broken. Take advantage of that opportunity because I can promise you there may come a time when you won't be able to. If there is absolutely no chance for you to reconcile with your father, the good news is that you can always reconnect to your spiritual father. God will never leave you or forsake you. Your destiny is and will forever be connected to the one person who knows the whole truth about who you are. Remember, God can see in you, what you can't see in yourself.

The most dangerous lies are the ones we tell ourselves"

– RICHARD BACH

To all my Fathers ….

- **Be involved** – *Whatever they are interested in, immerse yourself in it. They will only thrive with your full involvement in their lives*

- **Listen** – *Never lose the ears of your children. Listen to them and they will listen to you.* Put away the cell phone and cut the TV off in order to truly hear your children.

- **Focus on the positive**- Our children are constantly attacked by the negativity of this world. Be the one positive force they can count on in a world designed to destroy them.

W.O.W. #20 LIVE IN TRUTH AND OBEDIENCE

Don't let pride or anger keep you from receiving God's redemption. As I reflect on my life, God must have known I would grow up without my father. Perhaps he had to live the life he led so I could live the life I have now. Breaking the cycle in absent fathers has and will forever be a part of my legacy. I know that how you start does not determine how you end. Even without my father, my faith in God and his love for me has always been the driving force for my success. As you journey through this life, know that God has never made a mistake, and he can use any situation for our benefit.

I know that greatness is in you and God can use you to make the world a better place.

The End & The Beginning

ACKNOWLEDGMENTS

———

I believe that life is our greatest teacher. The lessons we learn as we evolve and grow help to shape our personality, character, and self worth. In order for us to reach our full potential, we must be able to take our fears, failures, disappointments, and tragedies and turn them into our greatest victories. To do this, we need great people that are willing to help and guide us with wisdom, compassion, and love. I would not have been able to make it out of the difficulties I've faced without the help of others. Thank you to Pearl McPherson, Lee & Lavern Joyner, Beatrice Stringfellow for laying a foundation of love, strength, and family connection that helps me stand strong today.

This book would not have been possible if it were not for the strength, support, and love of my wife and daughter. Thank you both for allowing me the time to complete what I believe

God called me to do. It was a tremendous blessing to know that I had your support and encouragement throughout this process. You are my reasons for living and I love you both. Thank you to my mom (Wanda Jackson) for sacrificing and loving me so much. I will never be able to repay you for what you have done for me. You showed me how to believe in myself and you gave hope in times of despair. To my sister, Patrice, who first inspired me to write this book. Thank you for your prayers and for being a living example of strength and enlightenment for me. To all of my brothers and sisters who took the time to sit and give me their input, I so appreciate you. (Navin, Bernie, Laval). To my two best friends on the planet, Rohan Pinkney and Larry Paige. Thank you for always standing in the gap for me. The friendships we share have changed my life. Thank you to all of my aunts on both sides of my family who have stood in support of me from the beginning. To my bonus parents, Sylvia and Al, thank you for building a legacy and always being there to love and support me. I couldn't have done it without your consistent love and guidance. Thank you dad for being willing to restore our relationship and give me the answers that I had longed for over the years. It meant more to me than you will ever know.

The completion of this book would not have been possible without the phenomenal team at New Degree Publishing. Eric Koester, thank you for believing that my story could help others. Brian Bies, Chanda, Linda, Zoran, Leila and the entire team, thank you all for being so patient with me throughout the process. Your efforts and flexibility truly made this project exciting, meaningful and possible. You all deserve a raise. Thank you to everyone who was willing to share their experiences and be interviewed for the book. I so appreciated your transparency and openness during our time. David Miller, Dave Bonezzi, Marvin Williams, Patrick Patterson, Dionne Simmons, Mark McKinney, Larry Paige, Rohan Pinkney, Taryne Dismuke, Jerome Smalls, Alhamisi Simms, Khris Charity, Bernard Jackson, Laval Coley, Navin Mills, Teresa A. Joyner, Cheryl Witherspoon, Clyde Witherspoon, Melissa Witherspoon, Wadija Ricks, Sharon Joyner, Christal Harris, Lawrence Coley and so many others.

Finally, thank you to all the people who have given me encouragement during this past year and who took the time to pre-order this book. I do not take it for granted what you have done to help make the book available for others. Special thanks to everyone at Memminger Elementary School and my work family at the Flippen Group for believing in me.